Dr. Ishwara P.

Job Attitudes of Teaching Professional: A Study

CANADIAN
Academic Publishing

2015

Job Attitudes of Teaching Professional: A Study

Dr. Ishwara P

Associate Professor
Department of Studies and Research in Commerce
Mangalore University, Mangalagangotri, Konaje
Karnataka, India.

CANADIAN
Academic Publishing

2015

Price : $27.86

First Edition : 2015

ISBN : 978-1-926488-23-3

ISBN Allotment Agency : Library and Archives Canada (Govt. of Canada)

Published & Printed by
Canadian Academic Publishing
81, Woodlot Crescent,
Etobicoke,
Toronto, Ontario, Canada.
Postal Code- M9W 6T3
Phone- +1 (647) 633 9712
http://www.canadapublish.com

ACKNOWLEDGEMENT

On completion of this book, I have great pleasure and privilege to acknowledge the help and support received from a large number of individuals and institutions It gives me immense pleasure to express my sincere, deep and heartfelt gratitude to **Dr. V. Murugaiah**, Professor, Department of Studies in Business Administration, Kuvempu University, Post-Graduate Centre, Shivagangothri, Davangere for his scholarly supervision and guidance and consistent encouragement in carrying out this work. He has showered his extraordinary skills and research insights on me. I am highly indebted to him.

The Department of Studies in Commerce and Business Administration, Kuvempu University provided me an opportunity to learn Commerce and Management, which is a base for my research work, and it moulded my personality. I take this opportunity to express my gratitude to **Prof. J. Madegowda, Prof. G.T. Govindappa**, for their encouragement. My thanks are also due to **Dr. P. Laxmana** for his consistent encouragement.

I received a great deal of moral support in preparing the questionnaire from **Prof. P.S. Yadapadithaya** and **Prof. P. Pakirappa** Mangalore University. I am thankful them for their timely help.

I am greatly obliged to all the Post-Graduate University teachers who have provided me with the necessary data. I dedicate this work to my parents, without whose encouragement, I would not have been in this position.

I thank once again all my friends and well-wishers who have made this work possible. However, any omissions that might have crept in are mine and own the full responsibility.

- Dr. Ishwara P

ACKNOWLEDGEMENT

On completion of this book, I have [illegible] privilege to acknowledge the help and support received from [illegible] of individuals and institutions. It gives me immense pleasure to [illegible] and heartfelt gratitude to Dr. V. Nirmala, [illegible] Professor, [illegible] in Business Administration, [illegible] University, [illegible] Development for his valuable suggestion and [illegible] encouragement in carrying out this work. He has shown [illegible] insight ensured I am [illegible].

The Department of Studies in Commerce [illegible] Kuvempu University provided [illegible] Management, which is [illegible] I take this opportunity to express my gratitude to Prof. [illegible] Prof. B. L. Govindappa for their cooperation [illegible] for his consistent encouragement.

I received a great deal of useful support in [illegible] questionnaire from Prof. R.S. Yadapadithaya and Prof. P. T. [illegible] University. I am thankful to them for their time [illegible].

I am grateful [illegible] all the [illegible] who have provided me with [illegible] data [illegible] without whose encouragement I [illegible] in this book.

I [illegible] once again all [illegible] made this work possible. However, [illegible] own the full responsibility.

CONTENTS

CHAPTER - I
INTRODUCTION

Teaching is a noble and an extraordinary complex activity involving a range of skills, perceptions, attitudes, knowledge and sensitivity. Thus, teachers must be more than mere technical or subject experts. A teacher's growth is reflected in his or her attitude, philosophy, values, belief and interests. Moreover, teacher's altitudes depend on their attitude towards teaching profession. Attitude of teachers is very important because it affects job behaviour. Job attitude is a mental state of the teachers towards job and its environment. Job attitudes are evaluative statements- either favourable or unfavourable. The Education commission reposed a great deal of confidence in teachers when it said that **"of different factors which influence the quality of education and its contribution to national development the quality, competence, job attitude and character of teachers are undoubtedly the most significant"**. For sustainable development of any nation, higher education is a major instrument of change. It has the important task of preparing leaders for different walks of life - social, political, cultural, scientific and technological. Universities function as the focal centre's of higher education. In addition to their traditional scholarly functions of teaching, evaluation and research, they now have the additional functions of extension and development also. They play a key role in the generation, transfer and application of new knowledge. The intellectual dynamism, resource fullness and economic prosperity of any nation are reflected in the quality of its university education. The challenge of the twenty first century is a challenge to survive as institutions of quality or excellence. The changing social and economic scenario all over the world indicates that flexibility, adaptability, capacity to bring about changes would be the need of the twenty first century.

The crucial role of higher education in the development and modernization of any society is well recognized. This is clearly enunciated and elaborated in many documents and reports. The statement of National Policy on Education, the subsequent document on the Programme of Action, reports of the planning commission and many others eloquently elaborate this point. Yet not much has been done to strengthen the higher education system and particularly its quality with a view to preparing the country for facing the challenges.

The Tenth plan for higher education has identified the following goals to be specially dealt with:

1. Relevance and quality of Education.

2. Access and equity

3. The universal and social change under which continuing education and women's studies are given special importance.

4. Management of Education, and

5. Finance.

Unlike single purpose, planning for education is relatively a much more complex task. This is because education encompasses multifarious objectives ranging from the development of physical, mental and intellectual abilities of the participants in the creation of the capability to learn on their own, from empirical experience intuitive perception and speculative thought. Moreover, education is also concerned with the inculcation of values among the participants. All these attributes eventually contribute synergically to the development of a capability and a dynamic worldwide, which results in tune with the demands of an ever-changing physical, technological and societal environment. Education leads to the formation of human capital and is an important investment for the development process (planning commission - 2003). Many traditional societies have deeply felt challenged by the typhoon of changes sweeping across the world. To meet the challenges four pillars of education were advised, they are;

(a) **Learning to know** or capacity to absorb new knowledge, whether the young person's mind are being trained so that throughout their lives they can continue to absorb the exploding knowledge that doubles every five years.

(b) **Learning to do:** means that the knowledge imparted to young people should also make them capable of gaining employment so that they become productive members of society.

(c) **Learning to live together**: that is education does not involve merely developing individual skills, it also needs to encompass the necessity for young people to become positive and integrated elements of their respective societies.

(d) **Learning to be**: that is education must contribute to the all round development of each individual mind and body, intelligence, sensibility, aesthetic sense, personal responsibility, Spiritual values. The holistic education must acknowledge the multiple dimensions of the human personality - physical, intellectual, aesthetic, emotional and spiritual.

In the past, the educational processes were not confronted with the kind of challenges, which have to be faced today. Today, technologies are changing much more radically and more rapidly than ever before. These technological changes are resulting in changes not only in tools, the infrastructure and the profiles of work related activities, but also organizational structures, demographic profiles and even the concepts associated with national identity and sovereignty.

Origin and Development of University System

English Higher Education in India began with the establishment of Hindu College in Calcutta in 1817. By 1855, there were 281 High Schools and 28 colleges. To regulate those three universities - Bombay, Calcutta and Madras - were established in 1857. The growth contributed unimpeded and by 1947, there were 20 universities, 591 colleges with 2,28,881 pupils. University Education Commission, 1948-49 (popularly known as Radhakrishna Commission) emphasized the need for setting up an apex body to co-ordinate the growth and development of education at the tertiary level and maintenance of standards in Education. Thus University Grants Commission (UGC) came into existence by an act of parliament in 1956.

Table - 1.1

Growth of Higher Education System (1947-2013)

Sl. No.	Particulars	Year		Growth Fold Increase
		1947	2013	
1.	Conventional Universities	20	624	31.2
2.	Colleges (Total)	591	37,204	62.9
	a) Colleges General Education b) Professional Colleges	459 132		
3.	Enrollment (Total)	2,28,881	2,15,01,154	93.9
	a) Colleges General Education b) Professional Colleges	1,83,238 45,643		
4.	Teachers (Total)	24,000	9,51,000	39.6
5.	Teacher pupil ratio	1:9	1:22	

Source: UGC Annual Report 2012-2013.

In the 1990s, states encouraged many Postgraduate Centres, Open, Regional, Linguistic and Mahila Universities, which are around 265 universities/institutions as on March 31, 2003 with 88.00 Lakh enrolment including 35.00 lakh women students i.e., 43.0 per cent. During the academic session 2012-2013, the total enrolment in all courses and levels in regular stream was 215.01 lakhs including 93.06 lakhs women students, constituting 43.28 per cent .The affiliated colleges have taken lion-share in providing more accommodation than universities, whereas universities are dominating in research and Diploma / Certificate Courses.

Table - 1.2

Student Enrollment: University / Affiliated College

Sl. No	Stage	University Depts./ University Colleges	Affiliated Colleges	Total Percent to grand total	Percentage in affiliated colleges	Percentage in University
1.	Graduate	19,39,170	1,65,30,509	1,84,69,679 (85.90)	89.50	11.50
2.	Post Graduate	7,22,023	18,89,643	26,11,666 (12.15)	72.35	27.65

3.	Research	1,39,079	41,495	1,80,574 (0.84)	22.98	77.02
4.	Diploma / Certificate	1,43,724	95,511	2,39,235 (1.11)	39.92	60.08
	Grand Total	**29,43,996**	**1,85,57,158**	**2,15,01,154 (100.00)**	**86.31**	**13.69**

Source: UGC Annual Report 2012-2013, pp. 248

Even after 50 years of independence, the demand for non-science and technology courses have much demand in the educational market. The economic reasons may be less investment or low cost for high and quick returns. The following table shows that arts faculty has take lion-share of students, next is science and commerce. Engineering and medicine are slowly picking up around 10.0 percent of the total. In the race of acquiring knowledge in performing arts, foreign languages, and physical education are at low ebb. Even in awarding doctorates also Arts and Sciences have taken big chunk. Very less research is found in Medicine and law.

Table-1.3

Student Enrollment - Faculty wise (2003-2004)

Sl. No.	Faculty	Total Enrollment 2003-04	Percentage to total 2003-04	No. of Doctorate degree awarded	Percentage to total
1.	Arts	8157308	37.94	5642	32.00
2.	Sciences	3992007	18.56	5607	31.80
3.	Commerce / Management	3762003	17.50	1305	7.40
4.	Education	741905	3.45	617	3.50
5.	Engineering / Technology	3333165	15.50	2098	11.90
6.	Medicine	752277	3.50	617	3.50
7.	Agriculture	103013	0.48	564	3.20
8.	Veterinary Science	29325	0.14	194	1.10
9.	Law	400815	1.86	159	0.90
10.	Others	229336	1.07	828	4.70
	Total	**21501154**	**100.00**	**17631**	**100.00**

Source: UGC Annual Report: 2012-13, pp. 249

In the span of 50 years of times, 14-fold increase in universities has taken place. Even smaller states also started their own state or central universities. In quantity-wise university system was grown in an appreciable way.

Table - 1.4

UGC Recognized Universities, March 31, 2013

Sl. No.	State	No. of Universities	Under State Legislation Act	Deemed Universities
1.	Andhra Pradesh	36	01	07
2.	Arunachal Pradesh	04	-	01
3.	Assam	14	-	-
4.	Bihar	17	01	02
5.	Chhattisgarh	18	-	01
6.	Goa	01	-	-
7.	Gujarat	37	-	02
8.	Haryana	20	-	05
9.	Himachal Pradesh	21	-	-
10.	Jammu & Kashmir	08	01	-
11.	Jharkhand	11	-	02
12.	Karnataka	26	-	15
13.	Kerala	12	-	02
14.	Madhya Pradesh	29	-	03
15.	Maharashtra	21	-	21
16.	Manipur	02	-	-
17.	Meghalaya	09	-	-
18.	Mizoram	02	-	-
19.	Nagaland	03	-	-
20.	Orissa	15	-	02
21.	Punjab	16	-	02
22.	Rajasthan	49	-	08
23.	Sikkim	05	-	-
24.	Tamil Nadu	22	-	29
25.	Tripura	02	-	-
26.	Uttar Pradesh	46	01	10

27.	Uttaranchal (Uttarakhand)	16	-	04
28.	West Bengal	22	-	01
29.	NCT of Delhi	10	-	11
30.	Pondicherry (Puducherry)	01	-	01
31.	NCT of Chandigarh	01	-	-
	Sub-total	**496**	**04**	**129**

Source: UGC Annual Report: 2012-13, pp. 201-210.   Total: 629

It is observed from the table- 1.1 that after independence a massive growth has taken place in higher education, resulted in a fourteen fold increase in the number of universities and colleges. Student enrolment has gone up by nearly 39 times. Teacher pupil ratio has also increased from 1:9 to 1:22. Despite tremendous development in the higher education system, developing countries in general are characterized by an abundance of unskilled and untrained labour, existence of under employment and "unemployed intellectuals" on the one hand, and serious shortages of persons with critical skills including highly educated professional manpower, technicians, top level management and administrative personnel, qualified teachers, and the like on the other. It is widely accepted now that social and economic development cannot be ensured by making provision for capital, raw materials, machinery, power, etc., unless sufficient attention is given to the role of the human factor in the development process. Education is one of the means for the participation in the labour force. Here education contributes most obviously to HRD, or in economic terms, to human capital formation. Education is meant for development of Human Resource.

Role of Education in HRD

Despite geographical, historical and cultural diversities, the developing countries in general are characterized by an abundance of unskilled and untrained labour, existence of under employment and "unemployed intellectuals" on the one hand, and serious shortages of persons with critical skills including highly educated professional manpower, technicians, top level management and administrative personnel, qualified teachers, and the like on the other. It is widely accepted now that social and economic development cannot be ensured by making provision for capital, raw materials, machinery, power etc. unless sufficient attention is given to the role of the human factor in the development process. Education is one of the means for developing the skills, knowledge and capacities of persons for the participation in the labour force. Here education contributes most obviously to HRD, or in economic terms, to human capital formation. In all countries the cost of education tends to raise relative costs in many activities of all industries, education is one of the most labour intensive industry, about 75.0 per cent of its costs are wages and salaries.

The concern in human resources development is not just on improving work and productivity but all aspects that are vital to the improvement of the welfare of the people and their active participation in the development process. It encompasses a whole array of social, economic and cultural variables. In India, high unemployment and / or poverty rates have persisted despite the provision of free education up to the university level because the output of the educational system has not fully corresponded to human resource needs. Such mismatch arises from the lack of co-ordination among human resource, education and planning. Education can be regarded as constituting the core of the resources development strategy in India. However, it is not education in the narrow sense of schooling, but a broad concept encompassing health, nutrition, employment, science and technology.

The government has implemented the minimum needs programme to ensure the universal satisfaction of such basic needs as elementary education, adult education and rural education.

It is believed that qualitative and quantitative expansion of educational opportunities was to accelerate socio-economic development which inter-alia contributed towards skill formation, increase in productivity and learning of new ideas and techniques and also to enhance the opportunities of social mobility among the privileged and under privileged.

Teachers and Human Resource Development

With all the economies of the world slowly going global, it becomes essential that over most precious national resource - the human resource - be properly geared for this globalization. If our nation is to compete successfully in this competition environment, our human resource has to be developed, trained and made into experts of all the necessary areas. Today we cannot survive by being 'Jack of all trades'. In this era we should be master not only in one but also in two or three areas at the same time. This is the reason why we find engineering doing management courses, chartered accountants doing law courses and so on. In other words, in order to increase the productivity of the nation, we have to increase the productivity of each individual. A deep analysis of all the basic productivity factors like output, input, labour, capital, technology, etc. reveals that more than half of these factors are related to the quality of the work force. To improve the quality of human input and to bring about the desired production behaviour in the work force, we have to improve the following personal and organizational characteristics.

1. Job Attitudes of the employee
2. Knowledge & Skills, and
3. Opportunities.

Management theory speaks about how these can be and should be improved after an employee joins an organization. The quality of education depends on the quality of teaching. Competent, committed and dedicated teachers are the greatest assets for any educational institution. Education as an instrument of change is difficult, complex, significant and of immediate requirement for the growth and development of the economy. Its effective use requires strength of will, knowledge, motivation, job attitude and dedication to work and thus applies to all kinds of education, particularly higher education. The primary purpose of education is to provide an opportunity to develop the potentials of the human resource.

Theoretical Framework of Job Attitudes
Job Attitude

Robbins (1996)[1] Attitudes are evaluative statements- either favorable or unfavorable-concerning objects, people, or events. They reflect how one feels about something. When I say, "I like my Job", I am expressing my attitude about work.

Breckler(1984)[2]Attitudes are not the same as values, but the two are interrelated. There are three components of attitudes: cognition, affect, and behaviour.

9

The cognitive component of an attitude is a person's beliefs about, or factual knowledge of, the focal object of the attitude. Affective component of an attitude is the emotional or feeling segment of an attitude (e.g. pleasant versus unpleasant); and behavioral component of an attitude is an intention to behave in a certain way toward someone or something (e.g., university policy and administration, relationship with colleagues, one's own work)

Keller(1997)[3] A person can have thousands of attitudes, but most of the research in organizational behaviour identified three important job related attitude. They are job satisfaction, job involvement and organizational commitment. These work related altitudes tap positive or negative evaluations that employees hold about aspect of their work and its environment.

Job Satisfaction

Porter (1962)[4] Job satisfaction is simply how people feel about their jobs and different aspects of their jobs. It is the extent to which people like (Satisfaction) or dislike (dissatisfaction) their jobs. Job satisfaction is an attitudinal variable. In the past, job satisfaction was approached by some researcher from the perspective of need fulfillment- that is, whether or not the job met the employee's physical and psychological needs for the things provided by work, such as pay (However, this approach has been de-emphasized because today most researchers tend to focus attention on cognitive processes rather than an underlying needs. The attitudinal perspective has become the predominant one in the study of job satisfaction.

Cherniss (1987)[5] Job satisfactions of employees is determined by three sets of variables: Job characteristics, Organizational characteristics, and Individual characteristics. Job characteristics refer to variable that describe the characteristics of job. Organizational characteristics refer to variables that describe characteristics of the organization in which the jobs are performed. Individual characteristics refer to variables that describe characteristics of the employees who perform the jobs.

In general, therefore, job satisfaction refers to an individual's positive emotional reactions to a particular job. It is an affective reaction to a job that results from the person's comparison of actual outcomes with those that are desired or anticipated or deserved.

Job satisfaction can be considered as a global feeling about the job (General Job satisfaction) or as a related constellation of attitudes about various aspects or facets of the job. The global approach is used when the overall or bottom line attitude is of interest, for example, if one wishes to determine the effects of people liking or disliking their jobs. The facet approach is used to find out which parts of the job produce satisfaction or dissatisfaction. This can be very useful for organizations that wish to identify areas of dissatisfaction that they can improve. Sometimes both approaches can be used to get a complete picture of employee job satisfaction.

Job-Involvement

Lodahl (1965)[6] Job-involvement is very central to work motivation and is an important measure of organization effectiveness. The phenomenon of job-involvement emerged from a factor analytic study of job satisfaction. The concept is defined as "The degree to which a person is identified psychologically with his work or the important of work in his total self-image.

Prof. Kanungo, (1979)[7] gave the motivational approach to work involvement, defining the term as "a generalized cognitive state of psychological identification with work insofar as work is perceived to have the potentiality to satisfy one's salient needs and expectations. Thus the involvement in work, according to the author, depends on the saliency of individual's needs and on the perceptions that he has about the need satisfying potentialities of work.

According to Bass (1965)[8] the conditions that strengthen job involvement are; opportunity to make decisions, the feeling that one is making important contribution to company success, self-determination, recognition and freedom to set one's own work place.

Schwyhart and Smith (1972)[9] have stated that the concept differs from organizational involvement and job involvement is defined as 'the extent of a person's psychological identification with the organization employing him. It is conceivable that a worker could be involved in his job without being either involved in his company or satisfied with his job'.

The various definitions of job involvement have a common of meaning, in that; they describe the job-involved person, as one for whom work is a very important part of life. He is one who is affected very much personally by his job.

Organizational Commitment

The concept of organizational commitment has been differently conceived by different social scientists. Buchanon (1974)[10] views commitment as a partisan, affective attachment to the goals and values of an organization, to one's role in relation to the goals, and values and to the organization, for its own sake, apart from its purely instrumental worth.

Porter et al. (1974)[11] explain organizational commitment as "the relative strength of an individual's identification with and involvement in a particular organization". It is a state in which an employee identities with particular organization and its goals, and wishes to maintain membership in the organization.

Meyer and Allen (1991)[12] noted that common to the various definitions of organizational commitment is "the view that commitment is a psychological state that (a) characteristics the employee's relationship with the organization, and (b) has implications for the decision to continue membership in the organization". Thus, regardless of the definition, "Committed" employees are more likely to remain in the organization than are "uncommitted" employees.   What differs across definitions is the nature of the psychological state being described. To acknowledge these differences Meyer and Allen applied different labels to what they described as three component of commitment: Affective, Continuance, and Normative.

Affective commitment refers to the employee's emotional attachment to, identification with, and involvement in the organization. Employees with a strong affective commitment continue employment with the organization because they want to do so. **Continuance commitment** refers to the employee's awareness that costs are associated with leaving the organization. Employees who have strong continuance commitment to an organization stay with the organization because they believe they have to do so. Continuance commitment can develop as a result of any action or event that increases the costs of leaving the organization, provided the employee recognizes that these costs have been incurred. **Normative commitment** refers to an employee's feelings of obligation to remain with the organization. Thus, employees with strong normative commitment will remain with an organization by virtue of their belief that it is the "right and moral" thing to do.

Student Evaluation of teachers (SET) Performance

Performance appraisal constitutes an important tool of Human Resources Development. Employees at all levels have to be appraised or evaluated in their walk of life as continuing basis. Such appraisal is vital both for the growth of the organization and the employee development. Performance Appraisal is also known by different names such as 'Evaluation of Employees' or 'Evaluation of Performance' or 'Measuring of Excellence' etc. The former name of this is 'Merit Rating'; Merit rating can also be called 'Employee Rating'.

May Field (1964)[13] defines performance Appraisal is simply "an attempt to think clearly about each person's performance and future prospects against the background of his total work situation".

Performance appraisal varies from one type of employees to another type of employees. It differs from technical employees to non-technical employees, teaching staff to Non-teaching staff, sales employees to plant employees. One of the primary considerations of an appraisal system is who should be the rater. The primary aspect is whether appraisal should be made by superiors or peers or subordinates or a committee.

In order to improve the quality of higher education the University Grant Commission (UGC) has been making efforts for the last many years some of which proved fruitful, whereas a lot of areas still need improvement or attention. Many commissions, committees as well as individual scholars have given alternative measures for enhancing the quality of education. One such measure has been the evaluation of teachers by the students from time to time. Some researchers have conducted studies on this issue and have highlighted the positive and negative attitudes of the teachers towards SET (Student Evaluation of Teachers performance)

Review of Literature

Review of existing studies in this field is presented in four broad categories, namely Job satisfaction, Job involvement, Organizational commitment and Student Evaluation of Teachers (SET) performance

Job Satisfaction

While there has been several Job satisfaction studies, very few of them are about the university teachers or academics in general. Due to this a few studies, which are not directly related to the university education, have also been reviewed. The Studies identified included those conducted by Gruneberg and startup (1978)[14] discussed about the relationship of University teachers overall job Satisfaction with turnover decision, along with research and promotional opportunities. The study reveals that teaching, research and promotional prospects positively correlated with the overall job satisfaction, but negatively correlated with turnover decision.

Titus Oshagbemi (1999)[15] set out to compare the results of single versus a multiple–item measures employed to investigate the job satisfaction of university teachers. To measure the level of overall job satisfaction of university teachers, respondents were asked to answer eighteen questions concerning overall job satisfaction. In order to measure the job satisfaction of university teachers on specific (particular) aspects of their jobs, eight basic elements were selected viz. teaching, research, policy of administration and management, present pay, promotions, supervisor behavior, co-workers behavior, and working facilities. The result reveals that slightly more than 50 Per cent of the respondents were satisfied with their jobs most of the time or all the time. The job satisfaction derived from particular aspect i.e. teaching, research and their colleague's behavior is very high i.e. respondents appeared to be very satisfied with their main tasks. They were moderately satisfied with some aspects i.e. head of unit's behavior, physical conditions and working facilities in their universities. They were clearly dissatisfied with administrative and managerial functions, their present pay, and their promotions.

14

Malinowska and Tabaka (1987)[16] set out to establish a general scale of job satisfaction or dissatisfaction for four professional groups (teachers, doctors, lawyers, engineers). They found that the general level of job satisfaction among the four professionals is similar, except for teachers, for whom it is slightly lower.

Pollard (1996)[17] found that the single-item indicator offered a less comprehensive explanation of job satisfaction then did the four or seven item indicators. Scarpello and Campbell (1983)[18], on the other hand, concluded that a single-item measure of overall job satisfaction was preferable to a scale that is based on a sum of specific job facets.

Herzberg (1966)[19] expounded the dual-factor theory of job Satisfaction which states that there are two groups of factors which determine job satisfaction or job dissatisfaction. Two-factor theory suggests that only job- content related factors (e.g. achievement, responsibility, the work itself) lead to satisfaction. On the other hand, job context – related factors (e.g. pay, security, and working conditions) lead to job dissatisfaction but not to job satisfaction.

King, N. (1970)[20] pointed out, the two-factor theory is not entirely clear, and the theory neglects the role of personal factors, such as age and education etc., in influencing job satisfaction.

Titus Oshagbemi (1997)[21] findings do not support Herzberg's theory, which says that the factors that lead to job satisfaction are separate and distinct from those that lead to job dissatisfaction. His findings support the situational occurrences theory which argues that any given factor e.g. the work itself or salary, can result in either job satisfaction or dissatisfaction. This means that overall job satisfaction could be improved if employers concentrate their efforts at both situational occurrences and situational characteristics rather than by either factor alone. In effect, both hygienic and motivator's can contribute to job satisfaction and job dissatisfaction.

Pay Satisfaction and Career Growth

De santis, et.al (1992)[22] Researchers have shown that pay satisfaction and the need for career growth are two of the most important predictors of job satisfaction, given their strong theoretical linkage to the formation of job attitudes. U.S. Merit System Protection Board, (1990)[23] studies have also shown that the deterioration of pay and lack of promotional opportunities are associated with job dissatisfaction of public employees and their tendency to leave the civil services. Kuhlen (1963)[24] study reveals that a correlation of .62 between rating of satisfaction and attitude towards career choice and expected permanency of career.

Spector (1985)[25] found a mean correlation of only 0.17 between level of pay and job satisfaction in three samples representing a heterogeneous collection of jobs.

Lawler (1971)[26] points out that "impossible to tell whether the relationship found between a variable and pay satisfaction is due to the effect of the variable studied or another variable."

Andrews and Henry (1963)[27] report that pay satisfaction is positively related to organizational level whereas Lawler and Porter (1963)[28] report that when pay level is controlled, the evidence suggests that pay satisfaction is negatively related to organization level.

According to Taylor and Vest (1992)[29] when deciding if employees are fairly paid, people look at both absolute and relative amount of pay. The results of their studies suggest that external comparison, such as workers in other organizations or other employers, might have lower pay satisfaction while personal comparison, such as relatives or house hold members, might tend to increase pay satisfaction.

Kovach (1993)[30] surveyed over 900 employees in manufacturing jobs across a number of industrial organizations in the USA to determine levels of pay and benefits and satisfaction level with each. He found, among other things, that in the area of pay, workers in private organizations received higher absolute levels and were more satisfied with their monetary compensation vis a vis workers in public organizations. In the area of benefits, however, the relationship reversed with public sector employees receiving more and indicating a higher level of satisfaction.

Rice, Phillips, and Mc Ferlin (1990)[31] reported a moderately large correlation between pay level and job satisfaction in a sample of mental health professionals, who all had the same job. In a homogeneous sample, people are likely to compare themselves to one another and quite dissatisfied if their salary is lower than that of others in the same job.

In a workforce, whenever the expectations of the individuals are met, they will be satisfied with their jobs. Fatehi (1979)[32] found out that the job satisfaction of managers are influenced by pay, autonomy, esteem and self actualization as well as management level. If organizational limitations do not permit an increase in the amount of pay, it may be possible to improve manager's satisfaction by increasing their autonomy.

Age

Research has shown that age and job satisfaction are related. The exact nature of the relation is not clear, as some studies have found a curvilinear, whereas others have found a linear relation.

Brush, Moch, and Pooyan (1987)[33] conducted a Meta-analysis of 19 studies that had a mean correlation of .22 between age and job satisfaction. These studies show that in general job satisfaction increases with age.

Zeitz (1990)[34] found a curvilinear relation in which job satisfaction declines early in life, levels off in middle age, and rebounds after approximately 45 years of age. Not all studies, however, have been able to find evidence for a curvilinear relation.

A factor that might be important in the age – job satisfaction relation is gender. Clark, Oswald, and Warr (1996)[35] have surveyed more than the 5000 men and women. They found clear curvilinear relations of age with job satisfaction, as well as the nature of work and pay satisfaction for men. For women the curvilinear pattern was small magnitude for general job satisfaction and did not exist for either factor.

Bedeian, Ferris and Kacimar (1992)[36] failed to find significant curvilinear trends might be, caused in some cases by relatively low statistical power due to insufficient sample size rather than linearity.

The researchers have also reported mixed results on the relationship of age and teachers job satisfaction. Srivastava (1986)[37] explored significant positive relationship of age and teacher's job satisfaction. Porwal (1980)[38] study reveals that age is not associated with job satisfaction of teachers.

Lewis and Gregory (1991)[39] Organizational behavior researchers have found that older employees are likely to develop a better fit between personal needs and jobs/organizations than younger employees.

Work Load

The Workload is defined as the demands placed on the employee by the job. Qualitative workload is the effort required by job tasks or the level of difficulty both mental and physical. Having to lift heavy objects and having to solve difficult mathematical problems both reflect qualitative workload. By contrast, quantitative workload is the amount of work that the employee must do.

Jex and Beehr, (1991)[40] workload has been found to correlate with job dissatisfaction as well as other job strains. However, correlation with job satisfaction has been inconsistent across studies. Dwyer and Ganster (1991)[41] found in a sample of manufacturing employees that the correlation between workload and job satisfaction was .37, whereas Spector (1987)[42] found a correlation of -.27 and -.17 with two different measures of job satisfaction. In a sample of clerical works, Jamal (1990)[43] found significant negative correlation of work load with job satisfaction. Karasek, Gardell, and Lindell (1987)[44] found that work load was negatively associated with job satisfaction and positively associated with heart disease. No significant correlation was found by Fox, Dwyer, and Ganster (1993)[45].

Rank

Oshagbemi (1997)[46], reported that overall job satisfaction was positively and significantly related to rank, but not gender or age. Professors were most satisfied with their overall jobs followed by Associate Professors, Senior Assistant Professors and Assistant Professors.

Bergmanns (1981)[47] administered Meta analysis satisfaction questionnaire to 1158 managers of three different organizations, revealed that structural characteristics of hierarchical level had the most significant positive effect on the manager's job satisfaction and also indicated a very strong relationship between satisfaction with personal progress and development and overall job satisfaction.

A Study of job satisfaction of 504 female Principals and 331 Vice-Principals in Texas public schools by Mary (1987)[48] found principals significantly more satisfied than vice principals and job tenure and job level did not show any significant effects on job satisfaction.

Whether the relation is curvilinear or linear, it is important to understand the reasons that age relates to job satisfaction. Older employees are more satisfied with their jobs than younger employee because they are more accepting of authority and expect less from their jobs. Other possibility is that older employees have better jobs and more skill than their younger counterparts.

Gender

Studies conducted by Dixit (1986)[49] reveals that sex has a significant effect on job satisfaction. Results reveal that female teachers had higher levels of job satisfaction as compared to male teachers. But a study conducted by Padmanabhaiah (1986)[50] explored no sex difference in job satisfaction.

Relations between gender and job satisfaction have been extremely inconsistent across studies. Greenhaus, Paasuraman and Wormley (1990)[51] found no significant gender differences in job satisfaction, even though the females in their study were less likely to have managerial or professional jobs and more likely to have lower-paid clerical jobs than the males.

Several explanations have been advanced to explain the equivalent job satisfaction of women to men despite nonequivalent job conditions and pay. It has been suggested that women may differ in expectations. Women expect less from work and so they are satisfied with less. Brush et al., (1987)[52] female employees may have developed over generations in which they had to accept fewer promotion opportunities and lower pay even for the same jobs.

19

Potential Effects of Job Satisfaction

There are many behaviors and employee outcomes that have been hypothesized to be the result of job satisfaction or dissatisfaction.

Job Performance

Conventional wisdom says that job satisfaction should be related to job performance. After all, a happy employee should be a productive employee. Studies have established that the correlation between the two variables is rather modest. Iaffaldan and Muchinsky, (1985)[53] in their two Meta-analysis found that job performance and job satisfaction correlate with one another, at least to a moderate extent. However, they do little to explain the reasons for observed correlation. Although it is possible that job satisfaction leads to job performance, the opposite direction of causality is also equally feasible. People who are happy with their jobs might be more motivated, work harder, and therefore perform better. There is strong evidence that people who perform better, like their jobs well because of the rewards that one often associated with good performance.

Jacobs and Solomon (1977)[54] hypothesized that the correlation between job satisfaction and job performance would be higher in jobs where good performance was rewarded than in jobs where it was not. Under such conditions, employees who perform well get rewards, and rewards should lead to job satisfaction.

Herzberg et. al., (1957)[55] study revealed weak relationship between job satisfaction and performance of employees.

Caldwell and O'Reilly (1990)[56] provided indirect evidence that job performance can lead to job satisfaction. They showed that matching employee abilities to job requirement enhance job performance. They also found that matching employees' abilities to job requirements enhances job satisfaction, as well. People who are better, able to do their jobs well, and perform well tend to have higher job satisfaction.

Organizational Citizenship Behavior (OCB)

Podsakoff et. al., (2000)[57] Organizational Citizenship Behavior (OCB) is behavior by an employee intended to help co-workers or the organization. Satisfied employees would seem more likely to talk positively about the organization, help others, and go beyond the normal expectations in their job. Moreover, satisfied employee might be more prone to go beyond the call of duty because they want to reciprocate their positive experiences. Consistent with this thinking, early discussion of OCB assumed that it was closely linked with satisfaction.

Schnake (1991)[58] stated that in contrast to job performance, OCB is behaviour that goes beyond the formal requirements of a job. It consists of those voluntary thinks employees do to help their co-workers and employers such as being punctual, helping others, making suggestions to improve things, and not wasting time at work. He hypothesized that OCB is caused by good treatment from the supervisor and by job satisfaction.

Life Satisfaction

The interplay of work and non-work is an important ingredient in understanding people's reactions to jobs. We tend to study, work mainly in the workplace, but employees are influenced by events and situations outside of their place of work.

Conversely, behavior and feelings about non-work are influenced by experience on the job. Life satisfaction refers to the person's feelings about life in general. It can be accessed on the facet level as satisfaction with specific areas of life, such as family or recreation. It can also be assessed generally, as overall satisfaction with life. Because life satisfaction reflects overall feelings about life, it is considered a measure of emotional well-being. Because work is a major component of life for people who are employed, it seems obvious that job satisfaction and life satisfaction should be related. Weaver (1978)[59] study found that a person who is satisfied with the job is likely to be satisfied with life in general. The findings of research studies conducted by Judge and Watanabe (1993)[60] consistently show that job satisfaction and life satisfaction are moderately and positively correlated.

Job Involvement

Lodhal and Kejner (1965)[61] view, it is an indication of work commitment. Job involvement refers to the degree of psychological identification with one's work. It also relates to the level of the centrality of work in one's total self-image.

Katz and Khan (1966)[62] Job involvement is a necessary condition if an individual is to accept fully the organization demands placed upon by his membership in the organization. The degree of job involvement is related to the level of aspiration and also to the degree of internalization of organizational goals.

According to Bass (1965)[63] the conditions that strengthen the job involvement are: opportunity to make decisions, the feeling that one is making an important contribution to company success, self determination, recognition and freedom to set one's own work pace.

Jones et al. (1975)[64] "Job involvement was found to be positively correlated with age and length of time that a person has been on a job" where as Manheim (1975)[65] found no relationship between them.

Rabinowitz and Hall (1977)[66] have presented the profile of a job involved person as one who is a believer in the Protestant Ethic, is older, has an internal locus of control, has strong growth needs, has a stimulating job, participates in decisions affecting him or her, has a history of success and is less likely to leave the organization.

Vroom (1962)[67] Job involvement relates positively with job performance for the non-technical employees.

Thoits (1992)[68] study shows that highly job involved employees derive substantial self-esteem from successful job performance. Russell and Cooper (1995)[69] Therefore, job performance may have a stronger impact on job related outcomes for highly job-involved workers compared with workers with a low level of job involvement who do not consider the job a central aspect of their self-concept.

Anantharaman and Deivasenapathy (1980)[70] found a manager and supervisors to be having more job involvement than workers.

In Babu and Reddy's (1990)[71] studies reveals that no positive association was found between high job involvement and positive attitude towards management. Similarly, personal and demographic characteristics such as age, education, marital status, and number of dependents, salary and tenure have not affected the job involvement.

Blau and Boal (1987)[72] have found that various combinations of organizational commitment and job involvement will have distinct consequences for organizations. In their study they designated the employees who exhibit both high organizational commitment and high job involvement (Institutional Stars), Employees with low levels of organizational commitment and job Involvement (Apathetic), Employees with high job involvement and low organizational commitment (Lone wolves), Employees with low job involvement and low organizational commitment (Corporate citizens).

Rabinnowitz and Hall (1977)[73] have suggested that job involvement should be examined from both the perspective of the individuals as well as work environment. They found that individual characteristics such as age, education, sex, tenure, level of control and values were linked it to job involvement. They also described job involvement was related to situational variables in the work environment such as head's behavior, decision making process, interpersonal relations and job characteristics as well as with work outcomes such as job satisfaction, job performance, turnover and absenteeism. Furthermore, they suggested that individual difference and job characteristic variables were about equally important in determining job involvement.

Organizational Commitment

Buchaman (1974)[74] examined the organizational commitment between government managers and business executives using a sample of 279 managers in three industrial and five governmental organizations. He defined organizational commitment as "a partisan affective attachment to the goals and values of an organization, to one's role in relation to goals and values and to the organization for its own stake, apart from its purely instrumental worth". The results of the study indicated that managers who felt they were making a real contribution to organizational success were more likely to develop commitment, and the experience had the greatest impact on commitment. Business executives typically reported more positive attitudes towards their organization than comparable government executives. This trend shows that business organizations are more successful at stimulating commitment to their purposes than government agencies.

Currivan, Douglas Brain(1998)[75] analyze casual relationships in a model of organizational commitment. "Organizational commitment is the degree to which an employee feels loyalty to a particular organization". Employee commitment is an important condition for organizational effectiveness. Their study provides a theoretical and methodological analysis of casual relationship in a model of organizational commitment. This study presents a model emphasizing the casual relationships among workplace structures and organizational commitment. Among the various workplace structures, the analysis reveals reutilization, co-workers support, supervisory support, and distributive justice exert the strongest influences on teacher commitment to their schools. Environmental conditions like Job opportunities and union participation consistently influence school commitment. The findings support a basic assumption that structural, environmental, and dispositional factors combine to shape employee's commitment to school. However the proposed model and findings provide no evidence that job satisfaction and organizational commitment are casually linked.

Leong, S.M, (1994)[76] study report that, overall, employees with strong commitment to organization work harder at their jobs and perform them better than those with weak commitment. Significant positive relations have also been reported between employees' commitment and their supervisor's rating of their potential for promotion and their overall performance on the job.

Bourants and Papalexandris (1992)[77] studied the differences in organizational commitment between managers in the private sector and in the public sector. Their results show that the commitment of managers' decreases along a continuum from private to publicly owned organizations. Managers report the existence of a gap between the perceived and the desired organizational culture in their firm, and this cultural gap tends to appear more in the public sector. Organizational commitment appears to be influenced negatively by the cultural gap. Therefore, this gap offers a plausible explanation for the lower commitment in public sector firms.

Yuch–Yun (1995)[78] studied relationships among teachers perceptions of empowerment, job satisfaction, and organizational commitment in public schools. The researcher surveyed 1114 teachers from 39 public schools. Pearson product moment correlation coefficients, stepwise multiple regressions and analysis of variance were used to analyze the data. The results indicated that teachers' perceptions of empowerment were significantly related to their job satisfaction and organizational commitments. The teachers who perceived higher level of empowerment had higher levels of organizational commitment. Among the demographic variables gender was found to be positively related to teacher's job satisfaction and their commitment to the organization, although the relationship is very weak. Finally, teaching position also had a weak and negative relationship with teacher empowerment, job satisfaction and organizational commitment.

Affective Commitment

Several studies reported that the organizational structure variables influence affective commitment. Bateman and Strasser (1984)[79] have found that decentralization of authority has been related to higher affective commitment. However the evidence regarding these links is neither strong nor consistent.

Konovsky and Cropanzano (1991)[80] have shown that the manner in which an organizational policy is communicated has also been linked to affective commitment. A higher affective commitment among employees who believed that the organization provided them with an adequate explanation for a new policy, the amount of information given and the sensitivity shown in organizational communication.

Research on personal characteristics has focused on two types of variables; demographic variables (e.g., Gender, age, tenure) and dispositional variables (e.g. personality, values). Overall, relations between demographic variables and affective commitment are neither strong nor consistent. Mathieu and Zajac (1990)[81] by giving their Meta-analytic evidence suggests that age and affective commitment are significantly, albeit weakly related; Although some studies have reported gender differences in commitment,

Aven, F.F.,(1993)[82] results of Meta analysis have shown that gender and commitment are unrelated.

As with employee age and gender, it is difficult to offer an unequivocal interpretation of the finding. It is possible that employees need to acquire a certain amount of experience with an organization to become strongly attached to it or that long-service employees retrospectively develop an affective commitment to their organization. Cohen (1993)[83] by giving his Meta analytic study reveals that the positive relation between organizational tenure and affective commitment. Alternatively, however, the correlation between tenure and affective commitment might simply reflect the fact that, overtime, those who do not develop strong affective attachment to the organization choose to leave it, and thus only the more highly committed employees remain among the longer-tenured group.

There is consistent evidence that individuals with particular personality characteristics are more or less likely to become affectively committed to an organization. Buchanan (1974)[84] study has shown that employees with a high need for achievement and a strong work ethic have stronger affective commitment.

Continuance Commitment

Continuance commitment refers to the employee's awareness that costs are associated with leaving the organization. Employees who have a strong continuance commitment to an organization stay with the organization because they believe they 'have to' do so. Continuance commitment can develop as a result of any action or event that increases the costs of leaving the organization, provided the employees recognise that these costs have been incurred. Meyer and Allen(1991)[85] summarised these actions and events in terms of two sets of antecedent variables, viz investment and alternatives.

The employee can make an investment in organizations in many ways, for example, by incurring the expenses and human cost of relocating a family from another city or by spending time acquiring organization-skills. Leaving the organization could mean that employees would start to lose or have wasted the time, money, or effort that was invested.

The other hypothesized antecedent of continuance commitment is the employee's perceptions of employment alternatives. Employees who think they have several viable alternatives will have a weaker continuance commitment than those who think their alternatives are few. Perceptions of alternatives can also be influenced by such things as the results of previous job search attempts, whether the organizations have tried to recruit the employee, and the extent to which family factors limit the employee's ability to relocate.

Allen and Meyer (1990)[86] found in their study that continuance commitment has been related to employee's perceptions about this transferability of their skills and their education to other organizations. In this study, employees who thought their education and training investment were less easily transferable elsewhere-expressed stronger continuance commitment to their current organization.

Lee (1992)[87] Employee's perceptions of employment opportunities that are available to them have been correlated with continuance commitment. His findings showed that employment opportunity negatively correlated with continuance commitment. This finding suggests that employees evaluate alternatives not only in terms of their availability, but also in terms of their viability for them personally.

Ferris and Aranya (1983)[88] used time based variables (e.g., age, tenure) as antecedent measure of continuance commitment. His study reveals that the perceived costs associated with leaving an organization will increase as they get older and increase their organizational tenure.

Normative Commitment

Mayer and Allen (1991)[89] defined Normative commitment is "an employee's feeling of obligation to remain with the organization". Thus, employees with strong normative commitment will remain with an organization by virtue of their belief that it is the "right and moral" thing to do. He has also been suggested that normative commitment develops on the basis of a particular kind of investment that the organization makes in the employee-specifically, investment that seem difficult for employees to reciprocate. These might include such things as organization sponsored tuition payments made on behalf of employees.

Rousseau (1995)[90] Normative commitment might also develop on the basis of the "psychological contract' between on employee and the organization. Psychological contracts consist of the beliefs of the parties involved in an exchange relationship regarding their reciprocal obligations. Robinson, S.L (1994)[91] unlike more formal contracts, psychological contracts are subjective and, therefore, might be viewed somewhat differently by the two parties. Psychological contracts are also subject the change over time as one or both parties perceive obligations to have been fulfilled or violated.

Ashforth and saks (1996)[92] In a study of newly hired school graduates, reported that normative commitment was related to organizational socialization tactics that provided employees with a more institutionalized (rather than individualized) set of early experiences.

Job Attitudes

Hendrik Daniel (1994)[93] has made a study on job attitudes of school principal of university of Pretoria (South Africa). The study reveals, lack of organizational commitment is associated with absenteeism and personnel turnover. An individual may be dissatisfied with his job environment, but may continue to produce acceptable work. Negative attitudes arise from personal problems, including physical, emotional, relationship problems and problems in the work environment. Negative attitudes are a cause for concern mainly because they have a detrimental influence on the progress of students. Negativism also affects interpersonal relationships of the teaching staff. The development of positive attitudes can be applied to each of the main managerial tasks of the principal. Although the staff development programme is seen as the ideal opportunity for changing or developing of positive attitudes, a new approach is used in the United States of America: organizational development. It is sometimes more beneficial for the entire school to bring about organizational change, than to attend to individual attitudes only. The empirical research programme proved that the principals balanced leadership style and recognition of teachers achievements are the main motivators for establishing positive attitudes among teachers.

Schafer, John Charles (1992)[94] has studied job attitudes of business teacher education in 'National Association for Business Teacher Education' (NABTE) and non-NABTE institutions and to ascertain if there were significant differences in three work attitudes – job satisfaction, job involvement and institutional commitment. A random sample of 140 NABTE business teacher educators and 90 non-NABTE business teacher educators were surveyed through questionnaire. Data furnished by the NABTE and non NABTE respondents included demographic characteristics of business teacher educator, their programs in institutions, and it identified similarities and differences. In summary, no support was found at the 0.05 levels for a statistically significant mean difference between NABTE and non NABTE business teacher educator according to their degree of Job Satisfaction, Job involvement, and institutional commitment.

Hammer et. al., (1981)[95] measures all three components job attitudes within a single sample, results show that correlation between job satisfaction and job involvement is 0.47, between job satisfaction and organizational commitment is 0.51 and between job involvement and organizational commitment is 0.37.

Brooke et al. (1988)[96] has provided empirical support for the discriminate validity of the measures of job satisfaction, job involvement and organizational commitment. The results of their study provide evidence that respondents are able to distinguish between the extents to which they like their job (satisfaction) the degree to which they are observed in or pre-occupied with their job (involvement) and the degree of attachment or loyalty they feel towards their employing organization (commitment).

Students' Evaluation of Teachers (SET) Performance

Wayne (1957)[97] study reveals that, In view of the purposes served by performance appraisal, 'who' does the ratings becomes more important. Different practices prevail across different organizations. The most commonly found raters include: immediate supervisor peers, subordinates, self and client served by the organization. He concluded that continuous appraisals with multi-raters using multiple instruments consisting of various performance dimensions would render the performance appraisal system more reliable, valid and acceptable. Austin and Cardy (1994)[98] Performance appraisal has long been regarded as one of the most critical yet troubling area of human resource management.

Arter, J.A., and Stiggins, R.J. (1992)[99] have noted the purpose of teachers evaluation are admission to training, certification, diagnostic feedback to teachers about the effectiveness of their teaching that can be useful for the improvement of teaching; accountability; administrative decision making; professional development; the selection of courses and instructors by students; and research on teaching. Their study also identified 'what is to be evaluated' classroom management, instructional skills, subject matter knowledge, and communication skills of teachers are evaluated.

Raths, J. (1982)[100] identified several methods and techniques used for teacher evaluation such as teacher interview; teacher command of the subject – matter; peer review; classroom observation; student rating; student achievement as a measure of teacher competence; indirect measures of teacher competence and faculty self evaluation.

Marsh and Dunkin (1992)[101] have extensively investigated the Student Evaluation of Educational Quality (SEEQ) instrument which was originally developed by Marsh. They used multidimensional perspective, multitract – multimethod and factor analyses, and constructivistic approach to study the dimensionality, reliability, generalizability, and validity of the SEEQ. They also compared the content of the SEEQ factors with general principles of teaching at higher education.

Tatro, C.N. (1995)[102] pointed out, faculty have several concerns about the appropriateness of using student ratings of instructor and instruction at all. He addressed the following concerns.

1. Students cannot make consistent judgment about the instructor and instruction because of their immaturity, lack of experience, and their capriciousness;
2. Only colleagues with excellent publication records and expertise are qualified both to teach and to evaluate their peer's instruction;
3. Most student rating schemes are nothing more than a popularity contest;
4. Students are not able to make accurate judgments until they have been away from course and university for several years;
5. Student rating forms are both unreliable and invalid; and
6. Extraneous variables or conditions that faculty think can affect student ratings.

De Ayale, R.J. (1995)[103] study reveals potential bias in students evaluation of teaching – course work load or difficulty, students' expected grades, rank of teachers, years of teaching experience, time of the administration of rating forms (i.e. mid-term or end – of – term), time of the day the course was offered did not affect the student's evaluations of teaching. In the same study, conflicting results have been obtained regarding the effects of gender of both students and teachers, class size and under graduate or post graduate levels of course.

Mandeep kaur (2001)[104] research study is based on the data collected from 100 teachers of Punjab Agricultural University, Ludhiana to study the attitude of teachers towards evaluation of teachers by students a five point opinion survey scale was developed. This study led to the conclusion that more than 53.0 per cent of the respondent teachers held that student alone are not capable to evaluate the teachers and more than 60.0 per cent of teachers admitted that students couldn't judge their teachers. The study further indicated that evaluation of teachers by the students will reduce the status of teachers, will undermine the autonomy of teachers as well as of the institution. The majority of them (73%) had the fear that it could be used as a means by the authorities to humiliate them and a large proportion (70%) also felt that it would not help them in knowing and improving their weaknesses and would not make the teachers less demanding. Respondents further felt that the university level (72%) is the most suitable level for the introduction of a teacher's evaluation by students and preferred that a committee should evaluate the teachers.

George Mathew (2001)[105] study reveals that teachers understand and accept the necessity of accountability through teacher evaluation by students and are not unwilling to submit themselves to such an evaluation, but they are not without their apprehensions about such a process; Consequently they feel it is too early to think of linking such evaluation to promotion. The findings of this study however, do provide a reasonable cause for optimism. If teachers can be convinced that the entire exercise is meant not to victimize them, but only to help them improve their professional efficiency, which in turn could raise the quality of higher education.

Based on existing reviews of literature, it could be stated that the measurement of overall job satisfaction of the employees different from measurement of specific job satisfaction. Organizational, Demographic and Career factors tend to influence job satisfaction, job involvement, and organizational commitment of employees. In turn, these jobs related attitudes tend to influence outcome variables such as job performance, life satisfaction, and organizational citizenship behaviour. It is also observed that, only a limited number of studies have been observed on job involvement when compared to the job satisfaction and organizational commitment. It is also found that job satisfaction, job involvement and organizational commitment are conceptually different from each other. It is worth nothing that most of the studies on university teachers relating to the job satisfaction. No authoritative and comprehensive studies relating to university teachers integrating job satisfaction, job involvement, organizational commitment and attitude towards Student Evaluation of Teachers (SET) performance have been reported so far. It is rightly pointed out by Morrow (1983)[106] these three job related attitudes have been included in the same study or measured simultaneously with in single sample.

Need for the Study

Job attitudes are of central interest to both researchers and practitioners. Employee attitudes can have bottom-line consequences for organizations as well as an important effect on the individuals who hold these attitudes. In the University set up the teaching and non-teaching staff are two broad categories of human resources. It is widely acknowledged that job attitudes of the teaching community will largely determine the quality of teaching and research performance on the one hand and the commitment to the teaching profession on the other. An extension of review of literature clearly indicated that there have been several job satisfaction studies, very few of them related to the university teachers or academics in general. However, no authoritative and comprehensive study has so far been done focusing on the job satisfaction, job involvement and organizational commitment of university teachers. A few existing studies have reported on job attitudes of industry and other personnel. However, the existing studies could not focus on job Attitude's of university teachers and this field of investigation remained as under researched till date. In view of this, it would be both an interesting and relevant proposition to make a genuine attempt to know what these university teachers feel about their organization, their expectation from job and job environment. The measurement and assessment of perceived levels of overall and specific job satisfaction, job involvement and organizational commitment of university teachers, identification of major determinants of their job attitudes. In addition to projecting and discussing the job related attitudes of university teachers, the present study would also expose the attitudes of university teachers towards Student Evaluation of Teachers (SET) Performance. Hence, this study entitled **"Job Attitude of Teaching Professionals-- A Case Study of University Teachers in the Karnataka state"** was undertaken with a view to abridging existing research gap.

Objectives of the Study

The central purpose of the study is to measure and assess the job related attitudes of university teachers in Karnataka state and raise certain major implication for higher education, leaning and teaching profession.

The specific objectives of the study are:

1) To study the organizational, demographic, and career-related characteristics of the university teachers.

2) To measure and assess the perceived levels of overall and specific job satisfaction, job involvement and organizational commitment of university teachers.

3) To identify and analyses of major determinant of job satisfaction, job involvement, and organizational commitment of university teachers.

4) To project the views and perception of university teachers towards the Student Evaluation of Teacher (SET) performance.

5) To offer pragmatic suggestions and recommendation for re-aligning the job Attitudes of university teachers based on the findings of the study.

Hypotheses

Based on an extensive review of earlier studies in this field the following research hypotheses have been formulated for further investigation in this study.

H_1: Overall job satisfaction of the university teachers tends to be significantly associated with their perceived level of specific job satisfaction.

33

H_2: There exists positive correlation between job satisfaction and job involvement; between job satisfaction and organizational commitment; and between job involvement and organizational commitment.

H_3: Organizational, Individual and Career factors tend to determine the perceived level of job satisfaction, job involvement, and organizational commitment of the university teachers.

H_4: There is no association between organizational, individual, and career aspects of the respondents and their attitude towards Student Evaluation of Teachers (SET) performance.

Methodology

The present study is based on the teachers working in various postgraduate departments of the conventional universities in the Karnataka state formed the sampling frame. Accordingly, Mysore University, Bangalore University, Dharwad University, Gulbarga University, Manglore University, and kuvempu universities are included for this purpose. However, other non-conventional universities such as technical, medical, agricultural, open and deemed universities were kept outside the purview of this study. This study is related only to the permanent (regular) university teachers; it does not include the guest and temporary faculties working in various universities mentioned above.

Population Distribution as on 31-3-2013

Universities	Assistant Professors	Associate Professors	Professors	Total
Manasagangotri, Mysore	143	102	105	350
Jnana Bharati, Bangalore	102	93	85	280
Karnataka, Dharwad	120	105	95	320
Jnana Ganga, Gulbarga	112	88	75	275
Mangalagangotri, Mangalore	72	45	53	170
Jnana Sahyadri, Shimoga	54	30	28	112
Total	603	463	441	1507

Source: University Prospectus

The Population included 603 Assistant Professors, 463 Associate Professors and 441 Professors regularly appointed by the universities are considered for the survey. The proportionate stratified random sampling technique used to choose the sample respondents. The stratification was based on the university wise and designation wise. An effort was made to choose 10 per cent of the population as sample size representing both university wise and designation wise.

It resulted in having a total sample size of 60 Assistant Professors, 47 Associate Professors and 45 professors; and ensured a fair and adequate representation of university teachers working in various postgraduate departments of conventional universities in Karnataka state. The particulars in respect of sample size and its distribution across different designation of university teachers are detailed in the following table.

Sample Distribution

Universities	Assistant Professors	Associate Professors	Professors	Total
Manasagangotri, Mysore	14	10	11	35
Jnana Bharati, Bangalore	10	9	9	28
Karnataka, Dharwad	12	11	9	32
Jnana Ganga, Gulbarga	11	9	8	28
Mangalagangotri, Mangalore	7	5	5	17
Jnana Sahyadri, Shimoga	6	3	3	12
Total	60	47	45	152

Tools

To study the job attitudes of university teachers Likerts opinion survey scale was used. In this study descriptive statistical tools i.e. percentage, mean and standard deviation and deterministic technique i.e. chi-square and correlation analysis used for the purpose of analyzing and interpreting the field survey data. Besides this, interesting findings were also projected in the form of charts, and diagrams.

Scope and Limitations

This study concentrated only on teachers working at a post - graduate level in the conventional universities of Karnataka State. Non - conventional universities such as agricultural, engineering, medical, open and deemed universities are excluded from the purview of this study. The research theme was exclusively focused on three basic job-related attitudes such as job satisfaction, job involvement and organizational commitment. In addition, this study also covers the attitudes of teachers towards Student Evaluation of Teachers (SET) performance. All undergraduate teachers were excluded from the scope of this study with a view to making an in-depth study of job-attitudes of postgraduate university teachers. To that extent, this is a 'micro study'.

It should be noted that the inference and conclusions of this research study may not be fully in conformity with the findings in respect of job attitudes of university teachers of other states in India or abroad due to regional and cross cultural differences and hence, cannot be generalized. In addition the job attitude of university teachers or any other employees in any organization may differ or change from time to time or period to period. Nevertheless, a general picture of the job attitudes of university teachers and the key determinants of such attitudes and their attitudes towards student evaluation of teacher's performance are presented in this study.

Chapter Outline

To facilitate, the present study has been divided into six chapters:

Chapter-I: Introduces the significance and importance of human resources in University. It also intended to provide nature of the topic, review of literature, objectives and hypotheses of the study. The sources and tools used for the collection and process of data, scope and limitation, and chapter outline are also given in this chapter.

Chapter-II: Focuses on brief profile of the various universities selected for this study. It also deals with the respondents Organizational, Demographic and Career characteristics.

Chapter-III: It provides a detailed account of the measurement and assessment of the perceived levels of overall job satisfaction and specific job satisfaction, expectations from job and job environment, and gap in job satisfaction of the respondents. It also touches upon the measurement and assessment of job involvement and organizational commitment.

Chapter IV: Identifies and analyses key organizational, demographic, and career related characteristics determining the perception levels of job attitudes of university teachers.

Chapter-V: Deals with the university teacher's attitude towards Student Evaluation of Teachers (SET) performance. It also verified the factors influencing to their perceived levels of attitude towards SET.

Chapter-VI: Concludes with the summary of the major findings and discussions presented in the earlier chapters. Some suggestions have also been offered to realign job attitude of the university teachers.

References

1. Robbins, S.P., (1996), Organizational Behaviour, 7th ed., Prentice- Hall of India Private Limited, New Delhi, pp. 180.

2. S.J. Breckler., (1984), "Empirical Validation of Affect, Behaviour, and cognition as Distinct Components of Attitude," Journal of Personality and Social psychology, pp.1191-1205.

3. R.T. Keller., (1997), "Job Involvement and Organizational Commitment as Longitudinal Predictors of Job Performance: A Case Study of Scientists and Engineers," Journal of Applied Psychology, pp.539-45.

4. Porter, L.W., (1992), "Job Attitudes in Management: Perceived Deficiencies in Need Fulfillment as a Function of Job Level," Journal of Applied Psychology, Vol.46, pp.375-384.

5. Cgerniss, S. and J.Kane., (1987), "Public Sector Professionals: Job Characteristics Satisfaction and Aspirations for Intrinsic Fulfillment Through Work," Human Relations, Vol. 40, pp.125-136.

6. Lodahl, T.M. and Kejner, M., (1965) "The Definition and Measurement of Job Involvement "Journal of Applied Psychology, Vol. 49(1), pp.24-33.

7. Kanungo, R.N., (1978), "The Concepts of Alienation and Involvement," Revisited Psychological Bulletin, Vol. 86(1), pp. 119-138.

8. Bass, (1965), "Organizational Psychology," Basten Allyn and Bacan.

9. Schwyharty W.R. and Smith P.G., (1972), "Factors in the Job involvement of Middle Managers," Journals of Applied Psychology, Vol.56, pp.227-237.

10. Buchanan. (1974), "Building Organizational Commitment: The Socialisation of Managers in Work Organization," Administrative Science Quarterly, Vol.19, pp.533-546.

11. Porter,et.al., (1974), "Organizational Commitment, Job satisfaction, and Turnover," Journal of Applied Psychology, Vol.59, pp.603-609.

12. Meyer,J.P. and Allen, N.J., (1991), " A Three – Component Conceptualisation of Organizational Commitment," Human Resource Management Review, Vol.1,pp.61-89.

13. May Field H.,(1964), "Defence of Personnel Appraisal," Management of Human Resource – Reading in Personnel Administration. New York: Mc-Graw-Hill, pp.305.

14. Gruneberg,M.M. and Startup .R.,(1978), "The Job Satisfaction of University teachers," Vocational Aspects of Education,Vol.30,No.76,pp.75-79.

15. Titus Oshegbemi., (1999), "Attitude Surveys, Studies, Statistical Analysis, Job Satisfaction," Journal of Managerial Psychology, Vol.14, pp 338-343.

16. Malinowaska –tabaka., (1987), "Complex Measures of Job Satisfaction /Dissatisfaction Among Professionals," Social Indicators Research, Vol. 19, pp.451-73.

17. Pollord . G., (1996), "A Comparison of Measures of Job satisfaction used in Studies of Social Communication," Gazette, Vol, 57, pp.111-119.

18. Scarpello.V. and Campbell. J.P., (1983), "Job Satisfaction: Are the parts there?," Personnel Psychology,Vol.36, No.3.pp.577-600.

19. Burke, R.J., (1996), "Are Herzberg's Motivation and Hygienes Unidimensional?," Journal of Applied Psychology, Vol.50, pp.317-321.

20. King.N.,(1970), "Clarification and Evaluation of the Two Factor Theory of Job Satisfaction," Psychological Bulletin ,Vol.74,pp.18-31.

21. Titus Oshegbemi., (1997), "Job Satisfaction and Dissatisfaction in Higher Education," Educational and Training, Vol.39, pp.354-360.

22. De santis, Victors, James.J. Glass, and Charldean Newell., (1992), "City Manager's Job Satisfaction and Community Problem Perceptions," Public Administration Review, Vol.52, pp.447-453.

23. U.S.Merit System Protection Board., (1990), "Why are Employees Leaving the Federal Government?," Public Personnel Management, Vol.21, pp.473-491.

24. Kuhlen,R.G.,(1963), "Needs, Perceived Need Satisfaction Opportunities and Satisfaction with Occupation," Journal of Applied Psychology. Vol.47, pp.56-64.

25. Spector, P.E., (1985), "Measurement of Human Service Staff Satisfaction: Development of Job Satisfaction Survey," American Journal of Psychology, Vol. 13, pp.693-713.

26. Lawler,E.E.,(1971), "Pay and Organizational Effectiveness : A Psychological View," Mc Graw-hill, New York.

27. Andrews, I.R. and Henry.M.M.,(1963), "Management of Attitudes Towards Pay," Industrial Relations,Vol.3, pp.29-39.

28. Lawler, E.E. and Porter, L.W.,(1963), "Perception Regarding Management Compensation," Industrial Relations, Vol.4, pp.41-49.

29. Taylor, G.S.and Vest M.J.,(1992), "Pay Comparisons and Pay Satisfaction Among Public Sector Employees," Public Personnel Management, Vol.21,No.4, pp.445-454.

30. Kovach, K.A., (1993), "Correlates of Employee Satisfaction with Pay and Benefits: Public/Private and Union/ Non-Union Comparisons," Journal of Collective Negotiations, Vol.22, No.3, pp.253-256.

31. Rice,R.W., Phillips, S.M., and McFarlin D.B.,(1990), "Multiple Discrepancies and Pay Satisfaction," Journal of Applied Psychology, Vol.75, pp.386-393.

32. Fatehi, K., (1979), "Factors Affecting Managers Job Attitudes," Industrial Management, Vol. 21, pp.5-9.

33. Brush,D.H., Moch,M.K., Pooyan, A.,(1987), "Individual Demograpic Differences and Job Satisfaction," Journal of Occupational Behaviour, Vol.8, pp 139-155.

34. Zeith,G.,(1990), "Age and Work Satisfaction in a Government Agency: A Situational Perspective,". Human Relations, Vol.43, pp.419-438.

35. Clerk,A., Oswald,A.,and Warr,P.,(1996), "Is Job Satisfaction U-Shaped in Age?," Journal of Occupational and Organizational Psychology,Vol.69, pp.57-81.

36. Bedeian,A.G.,Ferries,G.R.,and Kacmar,K.M.,(1992), "Age Tenure and Job Satisfaction: A Tale of two Perspective," Journal of Vocational Behaviour, Vol.40, pp.33-48.

37. Srivastava , S., (1986), "A Study of Job Satisfaction and Professional Honesty of Primary School Teachers with Necessary Suggestions," Fourth   survey of research in education, NCERT, Vol. II, New Delhi, pp.996-1000.

38. Porwal, N.K,(1980), "Personality Correlation of Job Satisfied Higher Secondary School Teachers," Third Survey of Research in Education, NCERT, New Delhi, pp.831-832.

39. Lewis, Gregory.B., (1991), "Turnover and the Quiet Crises in the Federal Civil Service," Public Administration Review, Vol.51, pp.145-155.

40. Jex,S.M., and Beehr,T.A., (1991), " Emerging Theoretical and Methodological Issues in the Study of Work Related Stress," Research in Personnel and Human Resources Management, Vol.9, pp.311-365.

41. Dwyer,D.J.,and Ganster,D.C.,(1991), "The Affects of Job Demands and Control on Employee Attendance and Satisfaction," Journal of Organizational Behaviour, Vol.12, pp.595-608.

42. Spector,P.E.,(1987), "Interactive Effects of Perceived Control and Job Stressors on Affective Reactions and Health Outcomes for Clerical Workers," Journal of Work and Stress, Vol.1, pp.155-162.

43. Jamal,M.,(1990), " Relationship of Job Stress and Type –A Behavior to Employee's Job Satisfaction, Organizational commitment, Psychosomatic Health Problems, and Turnover Motivation," Journal of Human Relations,Vol.43, pp.727-738.

44. Karasek,R.A.,Jr., Gardell,B., and Lindell,J.,(1987), "Work and Non Work Correlated of illness and Behaviour in Male and Female Swedish White Collar Workers," Journals of Occupational Behaviour , Vol.8, pp.187-207.

45. Fox,M.L., Dwyer, D.J., and Ganster,D.C., (1993), " Effects of Stressful Job Demands and Control on Physiological and Attitudinal Outcomes in a Hospital Setting," Academy of Management Journal , Vol.36, pp. 289-318.

46. Oshagbemi,T., (1997),"Job Satisfaction Profile of University Teachers," Journal of Managerial Psychology,Vol.12 No.1, pp. 27-39.

47. Bergmanns,T.J., (1981), "Managers and Their Organization: An Interactive Approach To Multidimensional Job Satisfaction," Journal of Occupational Psychology,Vol.54, pp.275-288.

48. Mary,F.B., (1987), "A Study of Job Satisfaction of Female Principals and Vice Principals in Texas Public Schools," Dissertation Abstract International, Vol.47(8), pp2881.

49. Dixit, M., (1986), "A Comparative Study of Job Satisfaction among Primary School Teachers and Secondary School Teachers," Fourth Survey Of Research in Education, NCERT, Vol. II, New Delhi, pp.932.

50. Padmanabhaiah,S., (1986), "Job Satisfaction And Teaching Efficiency Of Secondary School Teachers," Fourth   Survey Of Research In Education, NCERT, Vol.II, New Delhi, pp.1034-35.

51. Greenhaus,J.H., Parasuraman,S., and Wormley, W.M., (1990), " Effects of Race On Organizational Experience, Job Performance Evaluation, And Career Outcomes," Academy of Management Journal, Vol.33, pp.64-86.

52. Brush,D.H., Moch,M.K., and Pooyan, A., (1987), "Individual Demographic Differences And Job Satisfaction," Journal of Occupational Behaviour, Vol.8, pp.139-155.

53. Iaffaldano,M.T., Muchinsky.P.M., (1985), "Job Satisfaction And Job Performance: A Meta Analysis," Psychological Bulletin , Vol.97, pp.251-273.

54. Jacobs,R., and Solomon,T., (1997), "Strategies for Enhancing The Prediction Of Job Performance From Job Satisfaction," Journal of Applied Psychology, Vol.62, pp.417-421.

55. Herzberg, F.,Mausner,B., Peterson., (1967), Job Attitude: Revision, Responsibility and Opinions," Pitts Burgh Psychological Services of Pittsburgh, pp.162- 65.

56. Caldwell, D.F., and O' Reilly, C.A., (1990), " Measuring Person-Job Fit With A Profile Comparison Process," Journal of Applied Psychology, Vol.75, pp.648-657.

57. M.Podsakoff,S.B. Mackenzie., J.B.Paine and D.G. Bachrach., (2000), "Organizational Citizenship Behaviour: A Critical Review of the Theoretical and Empirical Literature and Suggestions for Future Research," Journal of Management, Vol.26, No.3, pp.513-563.

58. Schnake,M., (1991), "Organizational Citizenship: A Review, Proposed Model, and Research Agenda," Human Relations, Vol.44, pp.735-759.

59. Weaver, C.N., (1978), "Job Satisfactionas as A Component of Happiness among Males and Females," Personnel Psychology, Vol.31, pp.831-840.

60. Judge, T.A., and Watanable,S., (1993), "Another Look at the Job Satisfaction-Life Satisfaction Relationship," Journal of Applied Psychological, Vol.78, pp.938-948.

61. Lodhal T.M., and Kejner, M., (1965), "The Definition and Measurement of Job Involvement," Journal of Applied Psychology, Vol.49, pp.24-33.

62. Katz and Khan., (1960), "The Social Psychology of Organizations," Jhon,Wiley, New York.

63. Bass., (1965), "Organizationl Psychology," Bosten Allen and Bacon.

64. Jones A.P., JamesL.R., and Bruni J.R., (1975), "Perceived Leadership Behaviour and Employee Confidence in the as Motivated by Job Involvement," Journal of Applied psychology, Vol.60, pp.146-149

65. Manhum.B., "A Comparative Study of Work Centrality, Job Rewards and Job Satisfaction," Psychological Bulletin, Vol.84(2), pp.79-102.

66. Rabinowitz. S., and Hall.D.T., (1996), "Organizational Research on job Involvement," Psychological Bulletin, Vol.84(2), pp.265-288.

67. Vroom, V.H., "Ego Involvement, Job Satisfaction and Job performance," Personnel Psychology, Vol.15, pp.159-177.

68. Thoits, P.A., (1992), "Identity Structures and Psychological well Being: Gender and Marital Status Comparison," Social Psychology Quarterly, Vol.55, pp.236-256.

69. From.M.R., Russell,M., and Cooper M.L., (1995), "Job Stressors, Job Involvement and Employee Health: a Test of Identity Theory," Journal of Occupational and Organizational Psychology, Vol.68, pp.1-11.

70. Anantharaman R.N. and Deivasenapathy.P., (1980), "Job Involvement Among Managers, Supervisors and Workers," Indian Journal of Applied Psychology, Vol.17(2), pp.77-79.

71. Babu, P.P., and Reddy,K.S., (1990), "Job Involvement and its Relation to Attitude Towards Management," Indian Journal of Applied Psychology, Vol.27(1), pp.77-79.

72. Balu, G.T., and Boal,K.B., (1987), "Using Job Involvement and Organizational Commitment Interactivity to Predict Turnover," Journal of Management, Vol.15, pp.115-127.

73. Rabinowitz, S. and Hall,D.T., (1977), "Organizational Research on Job Involvement," Psychological Bulletin, Vol.84, pp.265-288.

74. Buchanan,B., (1974), "Government Managers and Business Executives, and Organizational Commitment," Public Administration Review, Vol.34(4), pp.339-347.

75. Currivan., and Douglas Brain., (1999), "An Analysis of Casual Relationship in A Model of Organizationl Commitment," Journal of Sociology, Industrial and Labour Relations, pp.298.

76. Leong,S.M., Randall,D.M., and Lote,J.A., (1994), "Exploring the Organizational Commitment–Performance Linkage In Marketing : A Case Study of Life Insurance Sales People," Journal of Business Research, Vol.29, pp.57-63.

77. Bourants,D., and Papalexandris,N., (1992), "Variables Affecting Organizationl Commitment : Private–Versus Publicly-Owned Organizations in Greece," Journal of Managerial Psychology, Vol.7(1), pp.3-10.

78. Yueh-Yun,W.V., (1995), Relationship Among Teachers Perceptions of Empowerment, Job Satisfaction, and Organizationl Commitment of Public Schools," Education ,Administration and Psychology, Vol.59(9), pp.148.

79. Bateman, T.S., and Strasser, S., (1984), "A Longitudinal Analysis of the Antecedents of Organizational Commitment," Academy of Management Journal, Vol.27, pp.95-112.

80. Konovsky, M.A., and Cropanzano, R., (1991), "Perceived Fairness of Employee Drug Testing as a Predictor of Employee Attitudes and Job Performance," Journal of Applied Psychology, Vol.76, pp.698-707.

81. Mathieu, J.E., and Zajac, D., (1990), "A Review and Meta –Analysis of the Antecedents, Correlates, and Consequences of Orgnisational Commitment," Psychological Bulletin, Vol.108, pp171-194

82. Aven, F.F., Parker, B., and Mc Evoy, G. M., (1993), "Gender and Attitudinal Commitment to Organization: A Meta –Analysis," Journal of Business Research, Vol.26, pp.63-73.

83. Cohen, A., (1993), "Age and Tenure in Relation to Organizational Commitment: A Meta Analysis," Basic and Applied Social Psychology, Vol.14, pp.143-159.

84. Buchanan, B., (1974), "Building Organizational Commitment: the Socialization of Managers in Work Organization," Administrative Science Quarterly, Vol.19, pp.533-546.

85. Meyer, J.P., and Allen, N.J., (1991), "A Three-Component Conceptualization of Organizational Commitment," Human Resource Management Review, Vol.1, pp.61-89.

86. Allen, N.J., and Meyer, J.P., (1990), "The Measurement and Antecedents of Affective, Continuance, and Normative Commitment to the Organization," Journal of Occupational Psychology, Vol.63, pp.1-18.

87. Lee, T. W., (1992), "A Study of Affective, Continuance, and Normative Commitment to the Organization," Unpublished Master Thesis, Sung Kyun Kwan University, Seoul, Korea.

88. Ferris K.R., and Aranya, N., (1983), "A Commitment of two Organizational Commitment Scales," Personnel Psychology, Vol.36, pp.87-98.

89. Meyer, J.P., and Allen, N.J.(1991), "A Three-Component Conceptualization of Organizational Commitment", Human Resource management Review, Vol.1, pp.61-89.

90. Roussean, D.M., (1995), Promises in Action: Psychological Contracts in Organization, (Newbury Park,CA:Sage).

91. Robinson, S.L., Kraatz, M.S.,and Rousseau,D.M., (1994), "Changing Obligations and Psychological Contract: A Longitudinal Study," Academy of Management Journal, Vol.37, pp.137-152.

92. Ashforth,B.E., and Saks,A.M., (1996), "Socialisation Tactics: Longitudinal Effects on Newcomer Adustment," Academy of Management Journal, Vol.39, pp.149-178.

93. Dutoit,Hendrik Daniel., (1994), "Changing the Attitude of Teachers as a Management Task of the School Principal" Education Administration, Vol.514, pp.3276.

94. Schafer, John Charles., (1992), "Job Attitudes of Business Teacher Educators in National Association for Business Teacher Education Institution and Non National Association for Business Teacher Education," Education Business Administration, Vol.52/10, pp.180.

95. Hammer,T.H., Landau,J.C., and Stern, R.N.,(1981), "Absenteesim when Workers have a Voice: The Case of Employee Ownershipm," Journal of Applied Psychology, Vol.66, pp.561-573.

96. Brooke,P.P., Russell, D.W., and Price, J.L.,(1988), Op.cit.

97. Wayne F.Cascio, (1987), "The Effect of Performance Discrepancies on Spervisors and Sbordinates" Applied Psychology in Personnel Management, Vol.34, pp77-81.

98. Austin,J.T., and Villanova,P., (1992), "The Criterion Problem :1917-1992" Journal of Applied Psychology, Vol.77, pp.836-874.

99. Arter,J.A., and Stiggins,R.J., "Performance Assessment in Education," Paper presented as part of the symposium- Performance Assessment methods: What can learn from Research in other professions? National meeting of the American Research Association, san Francisco.

100. Raths, J., (1982), "Evaluation of Teachers in Higher Education" Encyclopedia of Education research, Vol. 5, pp.611-618.

101. Marsh, H.W. and Dunkin,M.J., (1992), " Students Evaluation of university Teaching : A multidimensional Perspective", Higher Education – Handbook of Theory and Research ,Vol. III, pp.143-233.

102. Tatro, C.N., (1995), "Gender effect on Student Evaluation of Faculty," Journal of Research and Development in Education, Vol.28, pp.169-173.

103. De Ayala, R.J., (1995), "The Influence of Dimensionality on Estimation in the Partial Credit Model," Educational and Psychological Measurement, Vol.55, pp.407-422.

104. Mandeep Kaur., (2001), "Evaluating of Teachers by Student," University News: A weekly Journal of Higher Education, Vol.39 (15), pp.5-8.

105. George Mathew., (2001), "Teachers Attitudes Towards Evaluation of Teachers by Students," University News: A weekly Journal of Higher Education, Vol.39 (16), pp. 1-9.

106. Morrow,P.C., (1983), "Concept Redundancy in Organizational Research: A case of Work Commitment," Academy of Management Review, Vol.8, pp.486-500.

CHAPTER - II

PROFILE OF THE STUDY AREA

This chapter has been devoted to providing a brief profile of the respondents' employing universities, and their demographic, and career profiles. The **characteristics of the university** include certain variables such as NAAC status, age of the university, the size of the teaching workforce, and the number of student enrolment. The **demographic profile** of the respondents' includes age, sex, total monthly income, category/caste, marital status, personal health status, family structure, family size, household earner status, and distance from dwelling house to the workplace. The **career profile** of the respondents is analyzed taking into consideration of the department in which respondents work, work experience, status of doctoral research work, and work load (direct classroom teaching) per week.

The above variables of the respondents will be used as background information against which the results and discussions of the study are presented in the subsequent chapters.

UNIVERSITY PROFILES

MYSORE UNIVERSITY

The University of Mysore was established on 27th July 1916 by its founding father, His highness Nalvadi Krishnaraja Wodeyar, the then Maharaja of Mysore. It is the **SIXTH** University established in the country and the very **FIRST** in the Princely State of Mysore.

Mysore City, where the University is located, is the Cultural Centre of Karnataka. The City, which was the capital of Wodeyar Dynasty, the rulers of Mysore, is famous for its palaces, Temples, Gardens and Festivals. Tranquility and peace reign in this beautiful City, where the Arts are kept alive along hoary traditions. Being a splendid Tourist Resort with historical monuments and unique architecture, it is famous for silk, sandalwood oil and artifacts of ivory and sandalwood. The City has salubrious climate throughout the year. It is about 140 km south of Bangalore, the State Capital and is well connected by train and bus. The PG programmes of the University are distributed over three campuses. The main campus of Manasagangotri is in Mysore City, and the other two upcoming campuses are located in Mandya and Hassan. The Mandya Campus is called Sir M. Vishweshwaraya Post-graduate Centre, located at Thubinakere and is about 10km from Mandya on Mysore-Bangalore highway. The Post-graduate Centre at Hassan is called Hemagangotri, located at Kenchatahalli, 10 km from Hassan on Bangalore-Mangalore highway.

Institutional Evolution

The University gained in 1956, and in 1960, the Post-graduate Centre at the picturesque environs facing the beautiful Kukkarahally Lake was established. The revered National Poet, former Vice-Chancellor of the University of Mysore and a Jnana Peeth Awardee, Dr. K.V. Puttappa (Kuvempu), named the postgraduate campus as MANASAGANGOTRI. The Campus spread over 350 acres, has a serene atmosphere. The well-groomed trees that surround the buildings and the well-laid out avenues add to the beauty of the campus.

Originally the territorial jurisdiction of the University covered nine districts of the Karnataka State. With the carving out of Bangalore University (1964), Mangalore University (1980) and Kuvempu University (1987) the territorial jurisdiction of the University of Mysore are spread over to the four southern districts, viz., Chamarajanagar, Hassan, Mandya and Mysore.

Academic Programmes

The University of Mysore is an Affiliating University, covering both teaching and research, Higher education at post-graduate level and research are the main objectives of the University. There are seven faculties, viz., (1) Arts (2) Science and Technology (3) Commerce (4) Education and (5) Law (6) Engineering and (7) Medicine. In the last eight decades, the University has served the cause of Higher Education with distinction. Apart from 122 affiliated colleges (with 65,000 students), currently the University has 39 Postgraduate Departments and two Postgraduate Centres, offering nearly 60 postgraduate courses with strength of about 3,500 students on the campus with 319 faculty members and excellent co-curricular activities. Besides, there is a host of job-oriented Diploma and

Certificate Courses. The distinct strength of the University lies in providing high quality teaching and research with a strong focus on Pure and Applied Sciences, Humanities, Social Sciences, Languages, Law, Education, Physical Education, Fine Arts and Doctoral/Post-Doctoral Programmes. Most of the Postgraduate Departments are of international repute and known for excellence in research.

Centre for Information Science and Technology (CIST)

The University of Mysore has been in the forefront in extending non-formal education in Information Technology to the public through CIST, housed in the imposing Senate Hall Complex, Manasagangothri, Mysore. The CIST offers varieties of Certificate Courses encompassing several horizons of Information Technology, starting from entry-level basic courses. Students on the campus may also upgrade themselves with computer skills concurrently with their regular academic programmes, through the non-formal training packages offered by CIST and thus get themselves equipped to face the challenges of the modern world. This is an ISO 9001-2000 certified centre of the university.

Support Services

Library

The University Library located on the campus caters to the needs of students, research scholars and teachers of the University. There are nearly six lakh books that include 500 journals. More than 75,000 bound volumes of journals are available here. The Library provides the following services:

- In-house reference, consultation and home-lending
- Inter-library loan facility
- In-house photo copying facility
- Text book reference
- Text book loan service
- Internet browsing station with 128 KBPS capacity leased line currently with 18 nodes.
- CD-ROM (Computer Disk Read Only Memory) workstation extending quick information service about bibliographical references.
- Accession to online journals via UGC-INFLIBNET & JSTOR

The Library is kept open between 8.00 AM and 8.00 PM on all working days, throughout the year, except on special holidays. Departmental libraries are also available in some of the Post-graduate Departments.

Hostels

The University maintains two hostels for postgraduate women students and four hostels for postgraduate men students at Manasagangotri and Saraswathipuram. Hostel facilities are also available at the Postgraduate Centres at Mandya and Hassan.

Health Centre

A Health Centre is located on the campus to take care of the medical needs of the students, teachers and officials of the University.

Sports

A Separate Directorate of Physical Education looks after the sports activities. Vast sports fields, cricket stadium, tennis courts, gymnasium and a well-maintained swimming pool cater to the needs of sports-lovers of the City.

Student Welfare

A separate Directorate of Student Welfare looks after the student service programmes in the University. The students are encourages participating in co-curricular activities, such as literacy and Cultural Competitions, Inter-Collegiate and Inter-University Competitions. The State/Zonal/National/International Youth Festivals are also arranged from time to time. The Foreign Students Bureau is located at the Fine Arts College on the Manasagangotri Campus. This office provides guidance regarding admission to various courses and assists in all matters concerning foreign students and promotes cultural relations. A few foreign universities have entered into Memorandum of Understanding with the University of Mysore for teaching, research and cultural programmes. Students of Connecticut College, U.S.A. visit the University of Mysore to pursue their studies for a semester, as part of their academic programme.

Special Cell for SC/ST

There is a Special Cell to look after the welfare of SC/ST students. The cell also awards fellowships to students for carrying out research. Special coaching classes are conducted for the benefit of SC/ST students appearing for competitive examinations, such as IAS, KAS, IPS, NET and SLET. Training is offered in the application of computer techniques as well. Bridge courses are conducted for promoting communication skills, writing and oratory skills. The cell has a good library facility with looks on general knowledge and computers. Financial assistance is also provided to students of the Postgraduate Departments, through the State Directorate of Social Welfare.

Employment Information and Guidance Bureau

The University Employment, Information and Guidance Bureau, located in the University Library Building, provide information on courses and careers. Pamphlets and booklets are displayed at the Bureau Office. Lectures and Seminars are arranged in various colleges to highlight employment opportunities. The information about courses in other universities within the country and abroad is also provided. The professional and the postgraduate students can register their names for employment assistance at the Bureau.

BANGALORE UNIVERSITY

Bangalore University is one of the largest Universities in India Started as a 'Nucleus of Science' centre of Mysore University; it was endowed with the status of a University in 1964. Though originally intended to be a Federal University, comprising of leading institutions of higher education in the city, it eventually emerged as an affiliating University. It grew in size and variety enormously in a short time. Even after Medical and Engineering colleges were all taken away from it to form two specialized Universities recently, the Bangalore University still commands student strength of nearly 3,00,000.As many as 400 Colleges and over 70 Post-Graduate Departments, make it the largest University in India. The faculty consists of 102 Assistant Professors, 93 Associate Professors, and 85 Professors. Bangalore University also administers four constituent colleges of which the Central College and the University Visvheswaraya College of Engineering are justly famous all over the country.

The renowned Engineer-Statesman Sir M. Vishveswaraya, one of the first Bharat Ratnas, founded the engineering college in 1917. This is one of the oldest engineering colleges of the country and was entrusted to the Bangalore University. It was renamed as the University Vishveswaraya College of Engineering (UVCE) in 1976. The University has responded to the growing needs of society and added new courses in Bio-technology, Microbiology, Computer Applications, Fashion Design and Apparel Technology, Tourism Administration, Finance Accounting, International Business, Yoga - to name a few.

Support Services

Many facilities are available on the campus for student and staff support. They include separate hostels for men and women, central canteen, a student center, staff development college, shopping complex, health center and university employment and guidance bureau.

With the growth of consciousness among various communities of the need of spreading education among its members, communal hostels were started. In order to encourage students of the respective communities these hostels came to be started by community associations.

On-line Examination System

For the first time, Bangalore University has introduced online examination system starting with the five correspondence courses for Community Based Rehabilitation (CBR). The examinations of the post-graduate diploma and three certificate courses are held recently through online. With the success of the on-line system, the university proposed to extend it to other correspondence courses in the future.

Distance Education

Bangalore University Distance Education Council offered distance education at all levels. Most often regular mail, videos, and CD-ROMs are used as study materials. Often students are required to come to meet meetings at regional offices on specific weekends.

Library

The learning and teaching on the campus are facilitated by a well equipped central library. The library has more than two lakh volumes. Researchers and faculty members have accessed to computer facilities, e-mail, internet, CD-ROM and INFLIBNET facility. The science departments have well-equipped laboratories. Science instrumentation center, folklore museum, botanical garden are also available as a central facility to various departments.

Sports

Excellent sports facilities with expert coaching are provided to the student and staff. A massive indoor stadium with hi-tech systems is one of the unique facilities built on the campus. The sporting boys and girls have done well in Kokho, Cricket, Yoga, Adventure Sports etc., at the national and International level.

Scholarship and Finance

To resolve financial pressure and to motivate the students to excel in their studies and research many scholarships and financial assistance are provided. The SC/ST cell offers guidance and ensures the welfare of the students belonging to SC/ST groups and other minority communities.

KARNATAKA UNIVERSITY

Karnataka university is the second oldest but the largest of the 7 universities and two university status institutions in the state of Karnataka in South India. The university, which is 55 years old, is respected nationally and internationally for its academic standards. Having had its incorporation in March 1950 under the then Bombay state, it was transferred to the State of Karnataka in 1956 when the states were recognised on linguistic principles. Under the Karnataka State Universities Act 1976, all the universities in the state, including Karnataka University, have been brought under a uniform constitution and administrative structure. The university serves at present the needs of four district of North Karnataka, viz, Dharwad, Belgaum, Bijapur and Uttara Kannada, although after the reorganization of states, its jurisdiction extended to all the eight district of North Karnataka. Till 1980 the postgraduate centre at Gulbarga in the northern most part of Karnataka was under Karnataka University and it has been upgraded into the full-fledged Gulbarga University with Jurisdiction over the remaining four districts of North Karnataka.

Dharwad: Cultural Capital of Karnataka

Dharwad, the seat of the University, was a great intellectual and cultural centre even before India become independent, and in fact, it was in the Vanguard of the national struggle for freedom. It has continued to retain its heritage even now and next to Bangalore, the capital of the state. It is the nerve-centre of all intellectual, social, cultural and political activity. It has a salubrious climate, with mild summers (Max. Temp. 36°C) and mild winters (Min. Temp. 16°C) and has a moderate rainfall of about 88.90 cms.

It also offers undergraduate course at five constituent colleges, viz., Karnataka Science College, Karnataka Arts College, University College of Education to which is attached a secondary school for practicing purpose (University Public School), University College of Law, and University College of Music, which are directly administered by the University and which are located in a statellite Campus, at a distance of about 1 ½ kms towards the town.   In addition, the university has overseeing responsibility for undergraduate instruction, maintenance of standards, ensuring qualified faculty members and direct responsibility for the conduct of Examinations in 256 colleges spread over four district to which the privilege of affiliation has been granted after they have fulfilled the conditions laid down by the University.

The university has now two campuses, the main at Dharwad and the other at Belgaum, which is at a distance of about 80 kms towards Pune. In addition, there are two postgraduate centres located at Karwar and Bijapur. Both the postgraduate centres are unique in all respects and offer courses in Marine Biology (at Karwar), Art History and Tourism (Bijapur).

Dharwad Campus

The university has 41 postgraduate department covering almost all-important branches of knowledge from Anthropology to Zooloy at the Dharwad Campus. Faculty consists of 308 permanent teachers of which 63 Professors, 98 Associate Professors and 147 Lectures, supplemented by inviting eminent scholars to serve as guest faculty.

Belgaum Campus

In June 1982 the university opened a new campus at Belgaum where facilities are available for postgraduate studies and research leading to both Master's and Doctorate Degree programmes in seven disciplines viz., Kannada, Marathi, Economics, Commerce, Geography, Sociology and Mathematics.

The university has provided basic facilities at the Campus. Two hundred acres land has been acquired on Poona – Bangalore highway No.4. It is 20 kms away from Belgaum city. The university has constructed academic building at the cost of `. 75 lakhs. A hostel for students and a furnished guesthouse with well laid roads and independent water supply is provided. About 3 crores of rupees are invested to develop the campus and create academic facilities on the campus.

University Libraries

The university library is named after Prof. S.S. Basavanal, a well known literature of Karnataka and has on its shelues over 3,50,000 books and is receiving about 434 periodical publications. A separate textbooks corner for SC/ST students and IAS study corner are the feature of the library. The library has been designed United Nations Depository Centre where important United Nations documents are received regularly and are available for consultation.

Student Amenities

Hostels

There are six student hostels on the campus accommodating around 1200 students out of whom nearly 250 are lady students.

Health Centre

Moderately equipped Health centre has been functioning on the university campus for the last 30 years. This centre caters to large number of patients in a year (approximately 30,000 patients). A branch of health centre is also functioning in the Karnataka College Campus.

Employment Information and Guidance Bureau

The University Employment information and guidance Bureau was started in the year 1970 and has an employment exchange office of the government of Karnataka attached to it. An information and guidance cell is operating to cater to the needs of the students, parents and other interested public who seek information, and guidance regarding higher learning opportunities in India and abroad and regarding employment opportunities available through various avenues after graduation. The University Industry Centre started in 1989 is functioning in this bureau. This is making efforts to bring together.

University Scientific Instrumentation Centre

As the tempo of research work gathered momentum and the science departments felt the need for more sophisticated and costly equipment, the university established the scientific instrumentation centre with special financial assistance from UGC. The centre is housed in an independent building and has acquired several valuable equipments.

University Printing Press

The university runs a printing press for the printing work of the university as well as to meet the demands of publication of books based on research results. The text books in Kannada and other languages and the Journals are printed at the university press. Recently the printing press has been equipped with highly offset machines and DTP facilities. University and Industry to have collaboration to accommodate students during summer vacation in work exchange programme.

P.G. Gymkhana

It is a forum of the student of the university meant for promoting the sports and cultural potentialities among the students. The postgraduate Gymkhana can boast of noteworthy success at various competitions and meets including international cultural exchange programme (Japan) and National Youth Festival held at Bombay recently

GULBARGA UNIVERSITY

Gulbarga University was established in 1980 by an Act of Karnataka State. Its jurisdiction extends to the five districts of Gulbarga, Bidar, Raichur, Bellary and Koppal of Hyderabad Karnataka. Earlier it was a postgraduate centre of Karnataka University since 1970. The main campus is situated on 348 hectares of land, 10 kilometers east of Gulbarga City. It has 35 postgraduate departments and 4 postgraduate centres located at Krishnadevarayanagar, Bellary, Raichur and Bidar. Another postgraduate centre at Basavakalyan is on the anvil. The University enrolls about 3500 students every year for various postgraduate, M.Phil, and Ph.D. programmes in various disciplines. There are about 275 faculty members and about 700 technical and non-technical supporting staff. There are 165 colleges affiliated to this University, which enroll approximately 45,000 students every year in various graduate/diploma courses in arts, fine Arts, music, social sciences, science and technology, commerce, education and law.

Students and Other Services

Library

The university library has been ideally situated on the campus, easily accessible to all the departments. Over 2,00,000 volumes, 400current periodicals and many on CD-ROM database accessible on multi user CDNET are available. This library has been identified as one of the nodal centres of INFLIBNET programme by UGC for establishing nationwide networking of university libraries for resource sharing. A well-furnished INFLIBNET building has come up as an annexe to the university library. Multimedia facilities, Learning resources lab, Instructional material development centre, LAN, etc., are being established. Programmes on information skill management, Research communication and user education are organized for the benefit of students and research.

Computer Centre

The university has central academic computer centre and separate computers to MCA department, examination section, finance and administrative sections. There is a plan to network the university department and colleges affiliated to the university. Designing fabricating and testing of scientific apparatus necessary for research and teaching are the major responsibilities of the centre.

Science creativity centre-housed in USIC premises provides excellent opportunities to develop application oriented scientific and innovative technologies especially by the young.

Sports

Excellent sports facilities with expert coaching are provided to the students and staff. A massive indoor stadium with hi-tech systems is one of the unique facilities built on the campus. Many national and international tournaments are organized. Gym, Yoga and Adventure Sports Centres are the special facilities provided by the Physical Education Unit.

Scholarship and Finance

To resolve financial pressure and to motivate the students to excel in their studies and research many scholarships and financial assistance are provided. The SC/ST Cell offers guidance and ensures the welfare of the students belonging to SC/ST groups and other minority communities. Special Scholarships, Grants and other benefits are extended to these students.

Health Centre

Health centres on main campus and P.G. Centre, Krishnadevaraya Nagar have been established with modern facilities. Sophisticated X-ray unit, computerized auto-analyzer ECG and clinical laboratories have been installed for the benefit of staff and students.

College Development Council (CDC)

Coordinates planning and integrated development of affiliated colleges by providing the necessary help and guidance, CDC serves also as a link between the University Grants Commission of India, the University, the affiliated colleges and the State Education Department.

Student Welfare Office

This is one of the first points of contact in the university for students. "Students Grievance Window", a unique facility, looks into student's problems, under the personal supervision of the vice-chancellor. Many national and regional youth festival and cultural and literary programmes are organized periodically.

National Service Scheme (NSS)

NSS is a value -based voluntary student movement launched to provide the educated youth a meaningful forum for "development of personality through community service", it serves as a vehicle to take the campus to the community and make scholarship available on the campus to tackle the evils and problems of society around. During 1995 the unit won the prestigious "Indira Gandhi National Youth Award".

MANGALORE UNIVERSITY

The Government of Karnataka took a major academic decision to establish two new universities in Mangalore and Gulbarga in September, 1980 by amending the Karnataka State Universities Act, 1976. The Mangalore University Campus bears the poetic name Mangalagangotri. It is located about 20km to the South-east of the historic coastal town of Mangalore in the 350 acres of Wavy plateau, bald hillocks and green valleys, watching the timeless union between the river Nethravathi and Arabian Sea on the one side and the cloud-capped Western Ghats on the other. It grew out of the modest post-graduate centre of Mysore University to become the citadel of an independent university. In its triumphant decennial year the university made bold to propose a take-over of two government collages at Madikeri and Mangalore to nurse them back to academic health, and by 1993 they had become its constituent colleges.

There are 22 post-graduate departments on the university campus. They offer 27 Master degree courses, 17 in the Faculty of Science and Technology, 7 in the Faculty of Arts, 2 in the Faculty of commerce and 1 in the Faculty of Education and several P.G. Diploma course. Apart from the conventional course, non-conventional course such Materials Science, Bio- sciences, Marine Geology, Computer Software, Applied Botany,

Applied Zoology, Applied Chemistry and Yogic Science are offered. Nearly 900 students study on the campus. Girls outnumber boys in most of the departments, the ratio being 5:4.

Faculty consists of 118 permanent teachers, 22 professors, 40 Associate Professors, 56 Assistant Professors – Supplemented by inviting eminent scholars to serve as guest faculty.

The University has been First in the country to start an undergraduate programme of study on Hotel Management, Fashion Design, Garment Design, Leather design, Interior Decoration, Human Resource Development, Home Science and P.G. Diploma in Hotel Management. It is a pioneer in Launching paramedical course. It is one of the most important centres in the country today offering such paramedical course as Physiotherapy, Speech and Hearing, Pharmacy, Radiography, Medical Lab Technology, Nursing and Alternative Health Systems such as Ayurveda, Naturopathy and Homeopathy. The university has kept itself abreast with frontline areas of research and new courses of study arising from social demands. In a span of 20 years the university has awarded over 200 Ph.D., and 250 M.Phil., degrees.

Co-operation of industrial houses has been enlisted in certain major programmes of study such as post-graduate studies in Computer Software and Electronics

Library

The learning and teaching on the campus are facilitated by a well-equipped central library, which is housed in a sprawling and aesthetically appropriate building. It has over a lack of books besides Journals and their back volumes, reading room and audio-video and CDROM facilities. The library is computerized, where Internet facilities also available. The computer centre also adds to the sophistications of learning process, besides being the hub of specific teaching courses. The science departments have well-equipped laboratories. A science Instrumentation centre is also available as a central facility to various science departments, as does a Microtone Accelerator, which is designed as a national facility. There is a folklore museum, which captures the culture and ethnic character of the region. The campus also accommodates a botanical garden and a herbarium, which not only offers learning sites to student and researchers but also provide the much-needed green cover to the campus. The University College at Mangalore has library, which has a Goldman old books. Another constituent college of the university, Field Marshall K.M. Cariyappa College at Madikeri has been made a centre of study for Ecology and Environment, as it is located in a region rich in flora and fauna, which are not available elsewhere.

The university campus has a staff development college, which periodically organise Refresher course, Orientation course, Training Programme and HRD programmes for teaching and non-teaching staff. The department of sports and games that is running a post-graduate course has the necessary facilitates for indoor and outdoor games, a gymnasium and other resources.

Student Support and Progression

Many facilities are available on the campus for student support. They include separate hostels for men and women, a central canteen, a student centre with open air theatre and facilities for indoor games, a shopping complex which houses a co-operative departmental stores, a health centre with facilitating for nursery, facilities for photo copying, adequate facility for telecommunication, and university employment and guidance Bureau.

The university is also arranging campus interviews for placements. University has a Directorate for student welfare to guide the students in the matters of co-curricular and career progress.

A number of scholarships and fellowships are mobilized to encouraging deserving students.

Other Healthy Practices

Perhaps the healthiest practice which the university can boost is that it has respected the fundamentals. It has believed that teaching- learning is the most important culture it has guard and promotes to justify itself. That has ensured a smooth academic functioning of the university. Right from its inception it has adhered to the schedules specified in the calendar drawn up.

One of the unique features of the university area is that most of the subjects taught at the undergraduate level have their subject associations in which the teachers are members. These associations are for open academic discussions, debates and criticisms. They interact with the Boards of studies in matters like curriculum development, system of Examination and Evaluation. They act as a liaison between students and the university academic bodies, and provide the necessary feed backs.

The university has always endeavored to make-up its own inadequacies in resources and manpower by locating talents and finding initiative wherever available. Besides, the university has always made use of the expertise and talents available at the national and international levels.

KUVEMPU UNIVERSITY

Kuvempu University is one of the youngest of the affiliating type of Universities in Karnataka State and came into existence on 29-06-1987. It has been established, like other universities in Karnataka, under the Karnataka State Universities Act 1976. Kuvempu University was admitted to UGC fold under section 12 (B) of the UGC Act in September 1994. The territorial jurisdiction has been carved out of Mysore University's earlier Jurisdiction and the four revenue districts of Shimoga, Chitradurga, Davangere and Chikkamagalore constituent areas of Kuvempu University operation. Former P.G. Centres of Mysore University at Davangere and B.R. Project constitute the present P.G. Campuses of the Kuvempu University. The Head Quarters of Kuvempu University is located at Jnana Sahyadri Campus at Shankaraghatta, 28 kms from Shimoga city, the district head quarters and 18 kms from Bhadravathi, the well-known industrial town. The campus is only 2 kms from the magnificent Bhadra Reservoir across the river Bhadra, one of the important lifelines of the area. The main buildings of the university have been constructed on a small hillock, thus blending naturally with the landscape. The campus sprawls over an area of 230 acres. The entire campus area is free from any form of pollution including noise pollution. The main campus can be reached by using the private bus services. Shimoga, Bhadravathi and Tarikere towns are close to the campus and are well connected by rail.

Kuvempu University, named after the great humanist thinker and writer Sri. Kuvempu, was established to realize its institutional mission of creating through its varied academic activities a humanist, rational, scientific temper and a deep sense of commitment to the welfare of all sectors of society; to nurture and develop the regional sensibility to meet the demands of contemporary society; to protect and develop the rich environment of the area as well as the cultural, intellectual and political traditions which the university has inherited.

The main campus of the university extends to an area of 230 acres and the P.G. Centre campus at Davangere has an area of 73 acres. The university within a short period of 15 years has evolved into an important centre for higher studies with a wide range of academic programmes, which include 11 undergraduate courses and 25 post graduate course in the faculty of Arts, Science, Commerce, Business Management, Education, Physical Education, Computer Application, Fine Arts, Law, Library and Information Science. These include 18 programmes offered on the main campus five at post-graduate centre, Davangere and two in one of its constituent college (Sahyadri College, Shimoga). There are 128 affiliated colleges offering undergraduate programmes. About 32,000 students (13,493 girls and 18,303 boys) are pursuing various courses in the affiliated colleges. There are over 1,500 students in the university campus doing P.G/Ph.D programmes. The university has recruited 112 faculty members in permanent basis out of which 92 members possess Ph.D Degree, three M.Phil. The faculty consists of 28 Professors, 30 Associate Professors and 54 Assistant Professors. In addition to the permanent faculty, university has introduced the system of employing guest faculty teachers for maintaining the necessary standards in the matter of instruction.

The university offers 25 post-graduate programmes in the faculties of Arts, Commerce, Science and Technology. Certificate and Diploma course are offered in the faculties of Commerce, Arts and Science. The university has also been offering external degree facility at the undergraduate and postgraduate level.

The Choice Based Credit System (CBCS) could be introduced along with the semester pattern and it would provide adequate flexibility for the students in choice of course in consonance with their potentials and interests. The project work/Dissertation is compulsory components in the P.G programmes. The syllabi for various programmes are generally revised once in three years. In some of the fast changing disciplines such as Computer Applications, it may be even desirable to go in for more frequent revision, without sticking to the 3 year periodically. The curriculum offered at P.G. level is need based including the knowledge required for competing in national level exams like UPSC, KPSC, and NET etc.

The teachers are encouraged and supported to participate in seminars and conferences. The computer training for teacher is arranged by the university. The university is also made arrangement for Industry-University interface through collaborative teaching/research programmes with other centers /agencies. Department of Chemistry has an exchange programme with the University of Sunderland in the U.K as a part of collaborative research work.

Student Amenities

There are 2 hostels are well maintained at main campus accommodating around 500 students out of whom 200 are lady students. Canteen services are available in the campus. The P.G. centre at Davangere has quite an impressive and well-designed building complex of class room, hostels, guest house, etc. Moderately equipped health centre has been functioning on the university campus for the last 15 years.

Library

The library has more than 52,000 volumes and researchers and faculty member have access to computer facilities, e-mail, Internet, and CDROM and INFLIBNET facility. It is kept open on 365 days in a year from 8.00 am to 9.00 p.m. A separate textbook corner for SC/ST students is the feature of the library.

Sports

The sporting boys and girls have done well in Kokho, Kabaddi, Cricket, best physique, etc, at the state and national level. The sports and games facilities are available to the student at satisfactory level.

Student Support and Progression

The Environment in the University is conductive for the students to engage in studies. The university has counseling service and some of the departments have taken initiation to contact prospective employers and got placement for their outgoing student. The Alumni in the Departments are offering professional support to their respective departments by way of lecture and seminars.

Many students are recipients of Government of India Scholarships and Stipend. The SC/ST cell monitors the scholarships for the dalit students and also arranges some coaching programmes for competitive examinations. There are also some doctoral fellowships with financial support from university.

Since English proficiency is needed at the Master's level, remedial coaching classes to the students belonging to SC/ST and the economically weaker sections of the societies are conducted by the English Department.

Personal and academic counseling is being offered to the students in an informed way. There is an employment guidance bureau with a full time officer, supported by the government of Karnataka.

The university has constituted a research review committee to regularly by review the research work done and also scrutinise and recommend research proposals for financial assistance.

PROFILE OF THE RESPONDENTS

Organizational Characteristics of the Respondents

Table –2.1 deals with the classification of respondents based on their employing university characteristics such as NAAC status, age of the university, the total size of teaching faculty member, and the total number of student enrolment. All the 152 sample respondents are drawn from six conventional universities in Karnataka State.

Table - 2.1
Classification of the Respondents Based on Organizational Characteristics

Organizational Characteristics	Designation of the respondents			
	Assistant Professor	Associate Professor	Professor	Total
A. NAAC Status ***** (Five Stars)	36 (60.0)	30 (63.8)	29 (64.4)	95 (62.5)
**** (Four Stars)	18 (30.0)	14 (29.8)	13 (28.9)	45 (29.6)
***(Three Stars)	6 (10.0)	3 (6.4)	3 (6.7)	12 (7.9)
Total	60 (100.0)	47 (100.0)	45 (100.0)	152 (100.0)
B. Age of the University (in years) Up to 15	6 (10.0)	3 (6.4)	3 (6.7)	12 (7.9)
16-30	18 (30.0)	14 (29.8)	13 (28.9)	45 (29.6)
30 and above	36 (60.0)	30 (63.8)	29 (64.4)	95 (62.5)
Total	60 (100.0)	47 (100.0)	45 (100.0)	152 (100.0)
A. Number of Teaching Faculty Members Up to 200	13 (21.7)	8 (17.0)	8 (17.8)	29 (19.1)
200-300	21 (35.0)	18 (38.3)	17 (37.8)	56 (36.8)
Above 300	26 (43.3)	21 (44.7)	20 (44.4)	67 (44.1)
Total	60 (100.0)	47 (100.0)	45 (100.0)	152 (100.0)
B. Number of Student Enrolment Up to 2000	13 (21.7)	8 (17.0)	8 (17.8)	29 (19.1)
2001-3000	11 (18.3)	9 (19.2)	8 (17.8)	28 (18.4)
Above 3000	36 (60.0)	30 (63.8)	29 (64.4)	95 (62.5)
Total	60 (100.0)	47 (100.0)	45 (100.0)	152 (100.0)

Source: Field Survey

Out of 152 respondents 62.5 per cent of them working in NAAC accredited five star universities, while 29.6 per cent employed in four-star universities. However, the sample respondents' serving at three star universities accounts for 7.9 per cent.

As far as the age of the universities is concerned 92.1 per cent of the respondents work in those universities aged more than 16 years. Only 7.9 per cent of the respondents work in the university, which is aged less than 15years. In respect of the size of the University based on number of teaching faculty members working, out of 152 respondents 123 (80.9 per cent) respondents work for those universities having more than 200 teaching faculty and 19.1 per cent of them work for those universities having less than 200 teachers.

With regard to the total number of students' enrolment in various postgraduate departments in the universities 62.5 per cent of the respondent work for those universities, whose enrolment is more than 3000 students. Out of 152 respondents only 19.1 per cent of them are work, which have student enrolment less than 2000.

In short, it is clear from the data supplied through table-2.1 that more than 50.0 per cent of the respondents belong to the five stars NAAC accredited, university aged more than 30 years, teaching faculty members range above 200 and student enrolment is greater than 3000.

Demographic Profile of the Respondents

Table-2.2 reveals the different features of the respondents on the basis of their demographic characteristics. It includes age, sex, category to which respondent belong to, marital status, total monthly income, personal health status, family structure, family size, house hold earner status, and distance from dwelling house to work place.

Table - 2.2

Demographic Profile of the Respondents

Demographic Characteristics	Designation of the respondent			
	Assistant Professor	Associate Professor	Professor	Total
A. Age Group (in years)				
Below 35	25 (41.7)	-	-	25 (16.4)
35-45	33 (55.0)	41 (87.2)	11 (24.4)	85 (56.0)
Above 45	2 (3.3)	6 (12.8)	34 (75.6)	42 (27.6)
Total	60 (100.0)	47 (100.0)	45 (100.0)	152 (100.0)
Mean Age	36	43	49	42
B. Sex				
Male	43 (72.0)	34 (72.3)	41 (91.1)	118 (77.6)
Female	17 (28.0)	13 (27.7)	4 (8.9)	34 (22.4)
Total	60 (100.0)	47 (100.0)	45 (100.0)	152 (100.0)
C. Category /Caste				
Scheduled caste	11 (18.3)	7 (14.9)	4 (8.8)	22 (14.4)
Scheduled tribe	23 (38.3)	4 (8.5)	6 (13.3)	33 (22.0)
Other backward classes	3 (5.0)	10 (21.3)	4 (8.9)	17 (11.1)
General	23 (38.4)	26 (55.3)	31 (69.0)	80 (52.5)
Total	60 (100.0)	47 (100.0)	45 (100.0)	152 (100.0)
D. Marital status				
Single	10 (16.7)	4 (8.5)	-	14 (9.2)

Married	50 (83.3)	43 (91.5)	45 (100.0)	138 (90.8)
Divorcee	-	-	-	-
Widow	-	-	-	-
Total	60 (100.0)	47 (100.0)	45 (100.0)	152 (100.0)
E. Monthly Income (in `.)				
Below 40,000	7 (11.7)	-	-	7 (4.6)
40,000-1.00,000	34 (56.7)	32 (68.1)	3 (6.7)	69 (45.4)
Above 1,00,000	19 (31.6)	15 (31.9)	42 (93.3)	76 (50.0)
Total	60 (100.0)	47 (100.0)	45 (100.0)	152 (100.0)
Mean Income	23,717	28,447	36,222	28,882
F. Personal Health Status				
Sound	60 (100.0)	45 (95.7)	45 (100.0)	150 (98.7)
Chronically ill	-	-	-	-
Physically challenged	-	2 (4.3)	-	2 (1.3)
Total	60 (100.0)	47 (100.0)	45 (100.0)	152 (100.0)
G. Family Structure				
Nuclear	51 (85.0)	45 (95.7)	38 (84.5)	134 (88.2)
Extended	9 (15.0)	2 (4.3)	5 (11.5)	16 (10.5)
Joint	-	-	2 (4.5)	2 (1.3)
Total	60 (100.0)	47 (100.0)	45 (100.0)	152 (100.0)
H. Family Size (in numbers)				
Below 3	2 (3.3)	1 (2.1)	3 (6.7)	06 (3.9)

3-5	48 (80.0)	45 (95.7)	34 (75.6)	127 (83.0)
6-8	09 (15.0)	1 (2.2)	06 (13.3)	16 (10.5)
Above 9	01 (1.7)	-	02 (4.4)	3 (2.0)
Total	60 (100.0)	47 (100.0)	45 (100.0)	152 (100.0)
I. House Hold Earner Status				
Single-Earner	38 (63.3)	34 (72.3)	30 (66.7)	102 (67.1)
Dual-Earners	20 (33.3)	13 (27.7)	13 (28.9)	46 (30.3)
Multiple- Earners	2 (3.4)	-	2 (4.4)	4 (2.6)
Total	60 (100.0)	47 (100.0)	45 (100.0)	152 (100.0)
J. Distance from Dwelling house to work place (in k.m.)				
Less than 5	31 (51.7)	24 (51.1)	25 (55.6)	80 (52.6)
5-10	10 (16.7)	13 (27.6)	13 (28.9)	36 (23.7)
More than 10	19 (31.6)	10 (21.3)	7 (15.5)	36 (23.7)
Total	60 (100.0)	47 (100.0)	45 (100.0)	152 (100.0)

Source: Field Survey

Out of 152 sample respondents 85 (56.0 per cent) belong to the age group of 35-45 years, while 27.6 per cent represented the age group of above 45 years. It should be noted that the respondents aged less than 35years accounts for only 16.4 per cent. The mean age of Assistant Professor, Associate Professor and Professor Respondents is 36, 43 and 49 years respectively, while the overall average ages of respondents were 42 years. From this it is clear that more than 50.0 per cent of the respondents are aged between 35 and 45 years.

Sex-wise classification of respondent's shows that out of 60 Assistant Professor Respondents 17 respondents (28.0 per cent) are female and 72.0 per cent are male. However, the female Professor Respondents' are only 8.9 per cent of the total respondents. Out of 47 Associate Professor Respondents 34 (72.3 per cent) are male and the rest are female. Overwhelmingly majority of the respondents (77.6 per cent) are male and 22.4 per cent are female.

The category-wise classification of respondents depicts that out of 152 respondent teachers about 36.4 per cent belong to scheduled caste and scheduled tribe. 11.0 per cent of the respondents belong to the Other Backward Classes (OBC). However, slightly more than 52.0 per cent of the respondents come under the general category. In short, the ratio of General category University teachers to all other category was 1:1.

As far as marital status of respondents is concerned, out of 60 Assistant Professor Respondents 10 (16.7 per cent) are unmarried and only 8.5 per cent (4 Out of 47) Associate Professor Respondents are unmarried. However, most of the respondents are enjoying married life.

With regard to the distribution of the respondents based on their monthly income, the monthly income of 69 respondents out of 152 (45.4 per cent) are in the income group of `.40,000 – 1,00,000 and 50.0 per cent of the respondents monthly income is more than `.1,00,000. Out of 60 Assistant Professor Respondents, 19 respondents (31.6 per cent) average total monthly income is more than `. 36,000. The mean monthly Income of the Assistant Professor, Associate Professor, and Professor Respondents is `.33, 717, `.88, 447, `1, 16,222 respectively.

As far as personal health status of the respondents is concerned, as high as 98.7 per cent of the respondents report that their personal health is sound. Hence, most of the university teachers enjoy sound health.

A family structure of the respondent shows that, out of 152 respondents 88.2 per cent belong to nuclear families, while 10.5 per cent belongs to extended families. Out of 45 Professor Respondents 2 (4.5 per cent) live in the joint family. Overall this trend indicates that the disintegration of joint family structure in India.

Classification of respondents based on number of members in their respective families, 127 respondents (83.6 per cent) out of 152, belongs to the family having members ranging from 3 to 5. From the analysis it obvious that as high as 94.1 per cent of the university teachers have a family size ranging from 3 to 8 members.

Household earner status indicates that the number of active earning members in a family, Out of 152 respondents 102 (67.1 per cent) report, as single earner households. Only 30.3 per cent of the respondents belong to dual earner (two earning members) status. Out of 60 Assistant Professor Respondents 20 (33.3 per cent) belong to dual-earner households. In short, most of the university teachers represent single earner families.

As far as distance from dwelling house to the work place is concerned, out of 152 respondents 80 (52.6 per cent) reside nearer to the work place (with in 5 k.m from their work place). 47.4 per cent of the respondents dwelling places are located above 5 k.m distance from work place. From this it is clear that the half of the respondents either reside at university residential quarters or nearer to the university campus.

Career Profile of the Respondents

Table 2.3 shows the distribution of respondents on the basis of their career profile. Some of the important career profile aspects like department in which respondents work, work experience, workload per week (direct classroom teaching) and status of doctoral research work are considered.

Table- 2.3

Career Profile of the Respondents

Career Profile	Designation of the respondents			
	Assistant Professor	Associate Professor	Professor	Total
A. Department of the Respondents				
Arts	23 (38.3)	17 (36.2)	16 (35.6)	56 (36.9)
Commerce and Management	18 (30.0)	14 (29.8)	4 (8.9)	36 (23.7)
Science	19 (31.7)	16 (34.0)	25 (55.5)	60 (39.4)
Total	60 (100.00)	47 (100.00)	45 (100.00)	152 (100.0)
B. Work Experience (in years)				
Below 10 years	39 (65.0)	1 (2.0)	1 (2.2)	41 (27.0)
10-15	18 (30.0)	23 (49.0)	03 (6.7)	44 (29.0)
Above 15	3 (5.0)	23 (49.0)	41 (91.1)	67 (44.0)
Total	60 (100.00)	47 (100.00)	45 (100.00)	152 (100.0)
C. Work load per week (in hours)				
Up to 10	-	-	11 (24.4)	11 (7.2)
11-14	18 (30.0)	36 (76.6)	27 (60.0)	81 (53.3)
Above 14	42 (70.0)	11 (23.4)	7 (15.6)	60 (39.5)
Total	60 (100.00)	47 (100.00)	45 (100.00)	152 (100.0)
D. Doctoral Research Work				
Not Registered	2 (3.3)	-	-	2 (1.30)
Working	18 (30.0)	-	-	18 (11.9)
Submitted	2 (3.3)	-	-	2 (1.3)
Awarded	38 (63.4)	47 (100.0)	45 (100.00)	130 (85.5)
Total	60 (100.00)	47 (100.00)	45 (100.00)	152 (100.0)

Source: Field Survey

36.9 per cent out of 152 respondents belong to Arts faculty, it include 23 Assistant Professor, 17 Associate Professors and 16 Professor Respondents. Working in Commerce and Management departments' represent 24 per cent of the total 152 respondents and 39.4 per cent work in Science departments.

With regard to work experience, out of 60 Assistant Professor Respondents 39 respondents (65.0 per cent) have a total teaching and research experience in the University less than 10 years. As high as 37.0 per cent of the 152 respondents report their experience is more than 15 years.

As far as workload (number of direct classroom teaching) is concerned 53.3 per cent of the respondents report that they have direct teaching class works in the range of 11-14 hours per week. Only 15.6 per cent of the Professor respondents out of 45 engage more than 14 hours per week.

Overwhelmingly, majority of the respondent's 130 (85.5 per cent) respondents have got Ph.D. degrees. Only 30.0 per cent of the Assistant Professor respondents out of 60 are presently working for their doctoral research work.

CHAPTER - III

MEASUREMENT AND ASSESSMENT OF JOB ATTITUDES

Measurement is a process of assigning weights to objects or observations. Abstract properties like intelligence, motivational level, and attitudes of the employee cannot be directly observed; one must infer them from the observation of presumed indicants of the properties. Measurements of attributes help us to know the intensity with which an attribute is expressed. Measurement of job attitudes on a regular basis provides managers or employers with valuable feedback on how employees perceive their job, job environment, working conditions, policy & administration etc,. Distorted perceptions lead to negative attitudes about the job and organization. It is important for management or higher authorities to know about attitudes of the employees because employees' behaviour is based on their perceptions and not on reality.

This chapter presents the result and discussions pertaining to the measurement and assessment of the job-related attitudes as perceived and reported by the university teachers. Important aspects covered in this chapter include.

♦ Measurement and Assessment of General or Overall Job Satisfaction of University teachers.

♦ Measurement of Specific Job Satisfaction (fulfillment of various facets of job and job environment).

♦ Measurement and Assessment of Expectations from Job and its Environment.

♦ Measurement of Gap in Specific Job Satisfaction.

♦ Measurement and Assessment of Job Involvement and Organizational commitment.

```
                          Job Related Attitudes

        ┌──────────────────────┼──────────────────────────┐
        ▼                      ▼                          ▼
      Job                    Job                  Organisational
   Satisfaction          Involvement               Commitment

   ┌──────────┐                      ┌──────────────┼──────────────┐
   ▼          ▼                      ▼              ▼              ▼
 Overall Job   Specific Job        Affective    Continuance    Normative
 Satisfaction  Satisfaction       Commitment    Commitment    Commitment

        ┌──────────┐
        ▼          ▼
     Motivating    Hygienic
      Factors      Factors

    Achievement      University   policy
    Recognition      and administration

    Advancement or   Supervision
    promotional
    opportunity      Inter-personal
                     relations
    Work itself
                     Pay
    Professional
    growth           Working
                     conditions
    Responsibility
                     Job security
    Creativity
                     Mentoring
    Involvement
                     Library facilities
    Research work
                     Clerical assistance
    Status
                     Team work
```

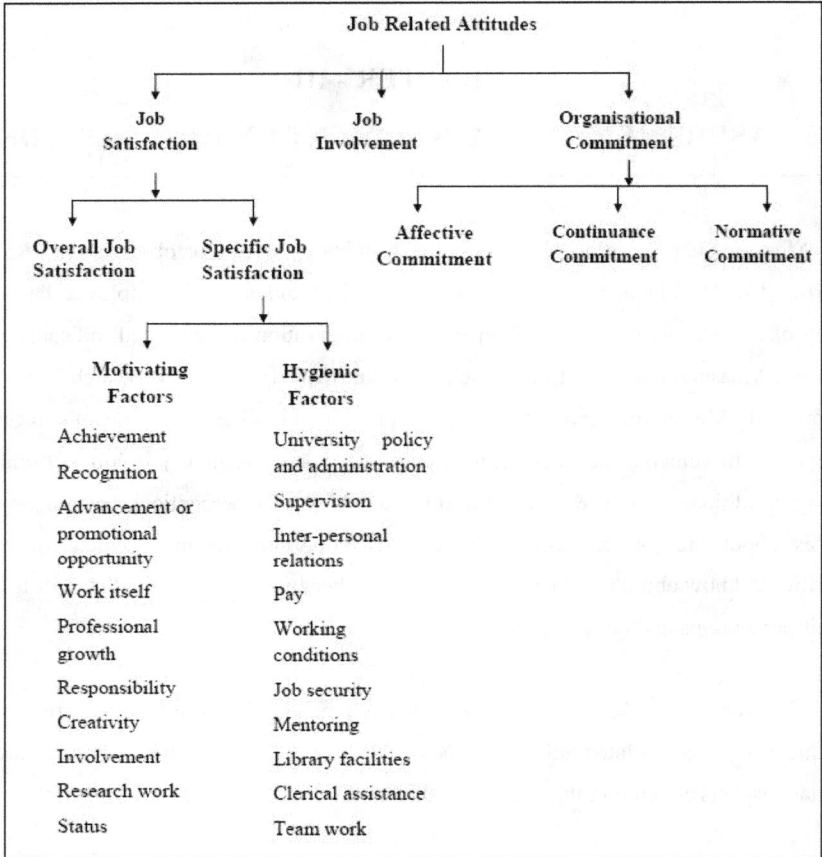

Source: Carl Heyel: Encyclopedia of Management of Management, pp.385.

Measurement and Assessment of Overall Job Satisfaction

In order to measure and assess the perceived levels of overall or general job satisfaction of the university teachers, eighteen items of overall job satisfaction scale has been used. It was developed by Bray field and Rothe (1951). The respondents were asked to indicate their perceived degree of agreement or disagreement in respect of the eighteen statements. The responses from every respondent to each item were scored by a five point agree or disagree scale. Accordingly, (5) for strongly agree, (4) for agree, (3) for neither agree nor disagree (2) for disagree, (1) for strongly disagree. The responses from every respondent summed up. Accordingly, the possible range of scores was between 8 and 90.

Higher score indicate the high level of overall job satisfaction and lower scores indicate low level of overall job satisfaction as perceived by the respondents. For a meaningful analysis, the possible range of scores was split into three categories as given below reflecting the levels of perceived overall job satisfaction.

Low   :   below 70

Moderate :   70-75

High   :   above 75

Table - 3.1

Overall (General) Job Satisfaction of the Respondents

Range of Scores and Levels of Degree	Designation of the respondents			Total
	Assistant Professor	Associate Professor	Professor	
Below 70 (Low)	26 (51.0)	17 (33.3)	8 (15.7)	51 (33.6)
65 – 75 (Moderate)	17 (32.7)	15 (28.9)	20 (38.4)	52 (34.2)
Above 75 (High)	17 (32.7)	15 (30.6)	17 (34.7)	49 (32.2)
Total	60 (100.0)	47 (100.0)	45 (100.0)	152 (100.0)
Mean Value	71.56	72.03	74.15	72.37
S. D.	6.40	11.03	10.16	6.41

Source: Field Survey

Table – 3.1 reveals that the respondents' perceived degree of overall job satisfaction based on their designation in the university. Of 152 respondents 33.6 per cent have perceived low level of overall job satisfaction, while the moderate and high level of overall job satisfaction as reported by the respondents account for 34.2 per cent and 32.2 per cent respectively. Of 45 professor respondents only 15.7 per cent of them perceived low level of overall job satisfaction, while the 26 Assistant Professor respondents out of 60 (51.0 per cent) reported low level of overall job satisfaction. In short, it is clearly indicated that 2/3 of the respondents perceived moderate and above moderate level of overall job satisfaction.

Measurement and Assessment of Specific Job Satisfaction

Based on the review of literature it is learnt that the measure of overall job satisfaction is distinct from the measure, which assesses specific job satisfaction. This distinction is mainly based upon the reasoning that all attitudes can be viewed at several levels of abstractness, ranging from an overall evaluation of the attitude object to very specific reactions to limited features of that object. Accordingly, in addition to the overall job satisfaction, an attempt is made to measure and assess twenty specific facets of job, which is originally developed by Frederick Herzberg in 1957. According to F.Herzberg's two-factor theory, the factors involved in producing job satisfaction are separate and distinct from the factors that lead to job dissatisfaction. These factors are classified into two categories.

Table - 3.2

Shows the Dissatisfiers and Satisfiers

DISSATISFIERS (Maintenance Hygienic factors, Job Context, and extrinsic factors)	SATISFIERS (Motivational, Motivators, Job content, intrinsic factors)
♦ University policy and administration.	♦ Achievement
♦ Supervision	♦ Recognition
♦ Inter-personal relations	♦ Advancement or promotional opportunity
♦ Pay	♦ Work itself
♦ Working conditions	♦ Professional growth
♦ Job security	♦ Responsibility
♦ Mentoring	♦ Creativity
♦ Library facilities	♦ Involvement
♦ Clerical assistance	♦ Research work
♦ Team work	♦ Status

Source: K.K. Unni, Indian Management (April 1976) pp. 47.

The above mentioned dissatisfiers and satisfiers are adopted in developing the questionnaire. Each item had its own five alternative response, scored from (1) strongly dissatisfied to (5) strongly dissatisfied. The data was collected for twenty specific areas of job and its environment. In this regard the respondents were asked to mention the present position of their satisfaction and also their expectations from job and its environment. Based on which gap in job satisfaction could be measured. Further, to discuss the problem in detail the responses of the respondents have been testified from two angles, that is based on designation of the respondents and NAAC status accredited to the respondents employing universities. Mean and Standard Deviation values were computed for all the factors to give the responses a clear shape and to make them comparative. These mean and S.D. values have been computed for all the three parts i.e. Fulfillment, Expectation and Gap.

The mean value for gap in specific job satisfaction is computed by subtracting fulfillment values from expected value, which indicates the extent of dissatisfaction towards specific aspects of job and its environment. The mean values are calculated on a five point scale which is originally used by Rensis Likert, where point three stands as midpoint, values more than three will be considered as the higher level of specific job satisfaction (fulfillment) and higher level of expectations from job. The values less than three will be treated as the lower level of specific job satisfaction (fulfillment) and expectations. As such, the findings relating to this part of the survey are broadly classified under three heads.

    A. Measurement of Specific Job Satisfaction (fulfillment of various aspects of job and its environment).

    B. Expectations from job and its environment.

    C. Gap in specific Job satisfaction

A. Measurement and Assessment of Specific Job Satisfaction (Fulfillment of Various Aspects of Job and its Environment):

Measurement of Specific job Satisfaction (fulfillment of various aspects of job and its environment) explains the feeling of a respondent for a particular aspect associated with his job and its environment. Thus, it represents the amount of a particular job satisfaction as perceived by the teacher.

The table–3.3 shows that, the specific aspects of job like, supervision, mentoring, library facility, clerical assistance, team work have mean values less than 3.00. On the other hand, the factors of higher fulfillment are work itself, pay, recognition for good work, achievement, research work, status, creativity, responsibility, professional growth, working condition and job security. Out of the twenty specific aspects of job, the respondents were

79

given least value to the 'clerical assistance' i.e. 2.684. The fulfillment level of all factors of job and its environment lies between the mean values of 2.684 and 3.967. Thus, it is concluded that most of the university teachers have reported their satisfaction of specific aspects of job and its environment on the higher side for the majority of the motivational or satisfaction factors.

Table- 3.3

Measurement of Specific Job Satisfaction

Sl. No	Facets of Job and Job Environment	Levels of Satisfaction					Mean Value	S.D
		S.S.	S	M.S	D.S	S.D.S		
1	University policy and Administration	7 (4.6)	56 (36.8)	50 (32.9)	30 (19.7)	9 (6.0)	3.145	0.986
2.	Supervision	6 (3.9)	45 (29.6)	39 (25.7)	46 (30.3)	16 (10.5)	2.862	1.082
3.	Inter-personal relations	17 (11.2)	70 (40.6)	29 (19.0)	29 (19.0)	7 (4.6)	3.401	10.633
4.	Pay	23 (15)	93 (61.2)	27 (17.8)	9 (6.0)	-	3.855	0.741
5.	Working conditions	14 (9.2)	57 (37.5)	40 (26.3)	31 (20.4)	10 (6.6)	3.224	1.081
6.	Job security	17 (11.9)	64 (42.1)	37 (24.0)	31 (20.0)	3 (2.0)	3.401	0.998
7.	Mentoring	4 (2.6)	31 (20.4)	67 (44.1)	38 (25.0)	12 (7.9)	2.849	0.926
8.	Library facility	8 (5.2)	34 (22.4)	60 (39.5)	41 (30.0)	9 (5.9)	2.941	0.971
9.	Clerical assistance	4 (2.6)	30 (19.7)	52 (34.2)	46 (30.3)	20 (13.2)	2.684	1.019
10.	Team work	8 (5.3)	36 (23.7)	45 (29.6)	46 (30.3)	17 (11.1)	2.816	1.082
11.	Achievement	23 (15)	71 (46.7)	47 (30.1)	9 (5.9)	2 (1.3)	3.684	0.849
12.	Recognition	16 (10.5)	76 (50.0)	42 (27.6)	12 (7.9)	6 (4)	3.553	0.926
13.	Advancement	16 (10.4)	44 (29.0)	62 (41.0)	25 (16.3)	5 (3.3)	3.27	0.973
14.	Work itself	31 (20.4)	89 (58.6)	28 (18.4)	4 (2.6)	-	3.967	0.704

Sl.		S.S.	S	M.S.	D.S.	S.D.S.	Mean	S.D.
15.	Professional growth	14 (9.2)	78 (51.3)	48 (31.5)	12 (8)	-	3.612	0.781
16.	Responsibility	15 (9.9)	83 (54.6)	37 (24.3)	17 (11.2)	-	3.632	0.811
17.	Creativity	17 (11.2)	72 (47.4)	40 (26.3)	13 (8.6)	10 (6.5)	3.48	1.023
18.	Involvement	13 (8.5)	79 (52.0)	38 (25.0)	20 (13.2)	2 (1.3)	3.533	0.876
19.	Research work	26 (17.0)	60 (39.5)	44 (29.0)	17 (11.2)	5 (3.3)	3.559	1.008
20.	Status	14 (9.2)	90 (59.2)	27 (17.8)	19 (12.5)	2 (1.3)	3.625	0.867

Source: Field Survey

S.S. = Strongly Satisfied, S = Satisfied, M.S.= Moderately Satisfied,

D.S. = Dissatisfied, S.D.S. = Strongly Dissatisfied.

Designation – Wise Classification

Table - 3.4

Shows the Mean Values of Specific Job Satification According to   Dsignation of the University Teachers

Sl. No.	Facets of Job and Job Environment	Designation of Respondents			
		Assistant Professor	Associate Professor	Professor	Overall Mean
1.	University policy and administration	3.383	3.000	2.978	3.145
2.	Supervision	3.017	2.723	2.800	2.862
3.	Inter personal relations	3.500	3.255	3.422	3.401
4.	Pay	3.783	3.681	4.133	3.855
5.	Working conditions	3.467	2.872	3.267	3.224
6.	Job security	3.233	3.319	3.711	3.401
7.	Mentoring	2.950	2.660	2.911	2.849
8.	Library facility	3.083	2.851	2.844	2.941
9.	Clerical assistance	2.717	2.681	2.644	2.684
10.	Team work	2.817	2.745	2.889	2.816
11.	Achievement	3.350	3.660	4.156	3.684
12.	Recognition	3.467	3.468	3.756	3.553
13.	Advancement	3.383	3.021	3.378	3.274
14.	Work itself	3.967	3.894	4.044	3.967

15.	Professional growth	3.700	3.574	3.533	3.612
16.	Responsibility	3.683	3.468	3.733	3.632
17.	Creativity	3.533	3.340	3.556	3.483
18.	Involvement	3.533	3.383	3.689	3.533
19.	Research work	3.383	3.511	3.844	3.559
20.	Status	3.500	3.532	3.889	3.625

Source: Field Survey

The overall and designation-wise mean values of specific job satisfaction are given in table - 3.4. From this table it is clear that, Professor Respondents have indicated the highest level of satisfaction for achievement (4.156), pay (4.133), work - itself (4.044), status (3.889), research work (3.844), and professional growth (3.533). The factors of lower fulfillment are clerical assistance (2.644), library facilities (2.844), mentoring (2.911) and supervision (2.800). The range of the highest and the lowest fulfillment (4.156 – 2.644) is 1.512, which is highest among all categories of teaching staff.

The factors like, supervision, working condition, mentoring, library facilities, clerical assistance, and teamwork are marked below mid- point by the Associate Professor respondents. The highly satisfied factors are work itself, pay, achievement, professional growth, status and research work. The range of the value maximum and the minimum specific job satisfaction in this category (3.894 – 2.66) is 1.234.

For the Assistant Professor respondents mentoring, teamwork and clerical assistance are less satisfied factors. The highest satisfied factors are work itself, professional growth, pay, and inter-personal relations. The range of highest and lowest satisfied aspects of job (3.967 – 2.717) is 1.25.

In short, the respondents of all the levels have indicated that mentoring, clerical assistance, and teamwork are less satisfied aspects of job and highest satisfied aspects of job are work itself, pay, professional growth.

NAAC Status-wise Classification

It is believed that fulfillment of the some aspects of job and job environment is greatly affected by the NAAC status accredited by the committee to various universities. Table – 3.5 shows that the mean values of respondents according to the NAAC status.

Table - 3.5

Shows the mean values of specific job satisfaction according to NAAC status of the university

Sl. No.	Various Facets of Job and Job environment	Universities' NAAC Status			
		***** Five Star	**** Four Star	*** Three Star	Overall Mean
1.	University policy and administrations	3.175	3.156	2.917	3.145
2.	Supervision	2.937	2.818	2.750	2.62
3.	Inter personal relations	3.413	3.351	3.667	3.401
4.	Pay	4.016	3.766	3.583	3.855
5.	Working conditions	3.365	3.130	3.083	3.224
6.	Job security	3.476	3.325	3.500	3.401
7.	Mentoring	2.810	2.870	2.917	2.849
8.	Library facility	2.825	3.00	3.167	2.941
9.	Clerical assistance	2.794	2.649	2.333	2.684
10.	Team work	2.762	2.844	2.917	2.816
11.	Achievement	3.873	3.610	3.167	3.684
12.	Recognition	3.714	3.519	2.917	3.553
13.	Advancement	3.413	3.208	2.917	3.274
14.	Work itself	4.048	3.922	3.833	3.967
15.	Professional growth	3.587	3.610	3.750	3.612
16.	Responsibility	3.762	3.468	4.000	3.632
17.	Creativity	3.508	3.519	3.083	3.48
18.	Involvement	3.603	3.545	3.083	3.553
19.	Research work	3.667	3.545	3.083	3.559
20.	Status	3.540	3.675	3.750	3.625

Source: Field Survey

The first group comprises of five star universities. The respondents of the five star universities have reported higher level of satisfaction (fulfillment) of various aspect of job and its environment are work itself, pay and other benefits, responsibility, research work, status etc. The respondents of four-star universities have indicated higher level of satisfaction for work itself, pay, status, achievement, professional growth etc. Similarly, three star university respondents reported higher level of satisfaction for work itself, professional growth, status, inter-personal relation's etc. A lower level of fulfillment is shared by many of the areas irrespective of the NAAC status are supervision, mentoring, clerical assistance and teamwork.

B. Expectation from Job and its Environment

In the questionnaire titled 'perceived importance' about various facets of job and job environment. The respondents were asked to mark their levels of expectations for various factors related to the present job. The overall mean values and standard deviations for various factors of job are given in table - 3.6.

The analysis of responses shows that, the mean values for the sample in all the cases were above four except in supervision. It means that the university teachers have claimed above mid-point aspiration level. The highest expectation is shown for Library facility, Achievement, Inter- personal relation, Research work, Working conditions, Work itself and University policy and administration. The range of the highest and lowest expectation of Job and its environment factors (4.664 – 3.914) is 0.75.

Table- 3.6

Level of Expetations from Job and its Enviornment

Sl. No.	Facets of Job and Job Environment	Level of exceptions of various facets of job					Mean Value	S.D
		H.E	A.M	M	B.M	L.E		
1	University policy and administration	89 (58.6)	56 (36.8)	4 (2.6)	1 (0.6)	2 (1.4)	4.507	0.709
2.	Supervision	32 (21.1)	90 (59.2)	18 (11.8)	9 (5.9)	3 (2.0)	3.914	0.861
3.	Inter-personal relations	101 (66.4)	44 (29.0)	5 (3.3)	2 (1.3)	-	4.605	0.621

84

No.	Item	H.E.	A.M.	M	B.M.	L.E.	Mean	SD
4.	Pay	80 (52.6)	67 (44.0)	5 (3.3)	-	-	4.493	0.564
5.	Working conditions	107 (70.4)	41 (27.0)	3 (2.0)	-	1 (0.6)	4.664	0.586
6.	Job Security	68 (44.7)	73 (48.0)	5 (2.6)	4 (2.6)	2 (1.3)	4.322	0.777
7.	Mentoring	69 (45.4)	56 (36.8)	16 (10.5)	6 (4.0)	5 (3.3)	4.171	0.995
8.	Library facility	113 (74.3)	36 (23.7)	2 (1.3)	1 (0.7)	-	4.717	0.523
9.	Clerical Assistance	75 (49.3)	55 (36.2)	11 (7.2)	10 (6.6)	1 (0.7)	4.273	0.906
10.	Team work	93 (61.2)	55 (36.2)	4 (2.6)	-	-	4.586	0.545
11.	Achievement	97 (63.8)	55 (36.2)	4 (2.6)	-	-	4.586	0.545
12.	Recognition	71 (46.7)	68 (44.7)	11 (7.3)	2 (1.3)	-	4.368	0.678
13.	Advancement	70 (46.0)	74 (48.7)	5 (3.3)	3 (2.0)	-	4.388	0.652
14.	Work itself	73 (48.0)	74 (48.7)	5 (3.3)	-	-	4.447	0.561
15.	Professional Growth	71 (46.7)	77 (50.7)	4 (2.6)	-	-	4.441	0.549
16.	Responsibility	79 (52.0)	69 (45.4)	4 (2.6)	-	-	4.493	0.552
17.	Creativity	64 (42.0)	79 (52.0)	8 (5.3)	1 (0.7)	-	4.355	0.613
18.	Involvement	61 (40.1)	80 (52.6)	10 (6.6)	1 (0.7)	-	4.322	0.626
19.	Research work	98 (64.4)	53 (34.9)	1 (0.7)	-	-	4.638	0.496
20.	Status	41 (27.0)	84 (55.2)	18 (11.8)	8 (5.3)	1 (0.7)	4.026	0.813

Source: Field Survey

H.E. = High Expectation, A.M. = Above Moderate, M = Moderate,

B.M. = Below Moderate, L.E. = Low Expectation

Designation - Wise Classification

Table - 3.7

Shows Mean Values of Expecations Based on Designation of the Respondents

Sl. No.	Facets of Job and Job Environment	Designation of the Respondents			
		Assistant Professor	Associate Professor	Professor	Overall Mean
1.	University policy and administration	4.600	4.298	4.600	4.507
2.	Supervision	4.017	4.000	3.689	3.914
3.	Inter personal relations	4.600	4.787	4.422	4.605
4.	Pay	4.417	4.511	4.578	4.493
5.	Working conditions	4.517	4.872	4.644	4.644
6.	Job security	4.350	4.319	4.289	4.322
7.	Mentoring	4.133	4.340	4.044	4.171
8.	Library facility	4.700	4.766	4.689	4.717
9.	Clerical assistance	4.117	4.383	4.356	4.273
10.	Teamwork	4.567	4.660	4.533	4.586
11.	Achievement	4.617	4.681	4.622	4.638
12.	Recognition	4.267	4.383	4.489	4.368
13.	Advancement	4.267	4.383	4.556	4.388
14.	Work itself	4.400	4.383	4.578	4.447
15.	Professional growth	4.517	4.255	4.533	4.441
16.	Responsibility	4.467	4.553	4.467	4.493
17.	Creativity	4.217	4.319	4.578	4.355
18.	Involvement	4.283	4.255	4.444	4.322
19.	Research work	4.533	4.702	4.711	4.638
20.	Status	3.850	4.021	4.267	4.026

Source: Field Survey

Table – 3.7 shows that the overall and mean value of expectations from job and job environment based on the designation of the university teachers i.e. Professor, Associate Professor and Assistant Professor.

The Professors respondents have a mean expectation 4.711 for research work, which is maximum expectation and followed by library facilities, achievements, and working conditions. For the Associate Professor respondents the highest level of expectation is expressed for congenial working condition (4.872) which is also the highest value in the whole table followed by research work, library facilities, inter personal relations. For the Assistant Professor respondents the highest and lowest levels of expectations are library facility (4.700) and status (3.850).

The range of mean expectations for the various factors of job are almost same for Associate Professor and Assistant Professor respondents (0.872 for Associate Professor and 0.85 for Assistant Professor) while the range of mean expectation of Professors is 1.022.

NAAC Status Wise Classification

Table – 3.8 shows the mean value of the expectations of respondents based on the NAAC status of the universities.

The respondents from five star universities have reported the highest level of expectation for all factors except supervision and status. The highest level of expectations is mentioned for library facility (4.825) and lowest level of expectation for supervision (3.857). On the other side, the respondents of the four star universities have indicated the highest expectations for working conditions (4.714). The range of means expectation of job and job environment is (4.714 - 4.013) 0.701.

The three star university teachers showed higher expectation for Working conditions, Library facility, University policy and administration, Inter- personal relations, Research work etc., The range of mean expectation for various factors is (4.750-3.583) 1.167.

Table - 3.8

Expectation from Job and Job Enviornment Based on NAAC Status

Sl. No.	Expectation from Job and Job Environment	NAAC Status			
		***** 5 Star	**** 4 Star	*** 3 Star	Overall Mean
1.	University policy and administration	4.492	4.494	4.667	4.507
2.	Supervision	3.857	4.013	3.583	3.914
3.	Inter personal relations	4.540	4.536	4.750	4.605

4.	Pay	4.476	4.519	4.417	4.493
5.	Working conditions	4.603	4.714	4.667	4.664
6.	Job security	4.270	4.390	4.167	4.322
7.	Mentoring	4.159	4.169	4.250	4.171
8.	Library facility	4.825	4.636	4.667	4.717
9.	Clerical assistance	4.238	4.325	4.083	4.273
10.	Teamwork	4.698	4.558	4.167	4.586
11.	Achievement	4.778	4.545	4.500	4.638
12.	Recognition	4.476	4.299	4.250	4.368
13.	Advancement	4.397	4.364	4.500	4.388
14.	Work itself	4.603	4.364	4.167	4.447
15.	Professional growth	4.492	4.416	4.333	4.441
16.	Responsibility	4.556	4.455	4.417	4.493
17.	Creativity	4.413	4.312	4.333	4.355
18.	Involvement	4.397	4.247	4.417	4.322
19.	Research work	4.746	4.571	4.500	4.638
20.	Status	3.952	4.104	3.917	4.026

Source: Field Survey

C. Gap in Specific Job Satisfaction

The gap between the levels of expectation and the present level of satisfaction of various aspects of job helps the management and university population to understand the possible avenues of improvement. It is assumed that higher the gap, greater the attention required to bridge it. It is essential to bridge the gap to enable universities to removal of dissatisfaction of their personnel and accomplish a higher level of expectations.

Table - 3.9
Show the Gap in Specific Job Satisfaction

Sl. No	Facets of Job and Job Environment	Gap in specific job satisfactions					Mean Value	S.D
		V.H.G	H.G	M.G	L.G	N.G		
1	University policy and administration	8 (5.26)	14 (9.22)	41 (26.97)	58 (38.16)	31 (20.39)	1.361	1.187
2.	Supervision	5 (3.29)	16 (10.53)	33 (21.71)	42 (27.63)	56 (36.84)	1.052	1.300

88

No.	Factor	V.H.G.	H.G.	M.G.	L.G.	N.G.	Mean	S.D.
3.	Inter-personal relations	4 (2.63)	24 (9.21)	29 (19.08)	40 (26.32)	55 (36.18)	1.203	1.203
4.	Pay	-	4 (2.63)	18 (11.84)	56 (36.84)	74 (48.64)	0.632	0.859
5.	Working conditions	9 (5.92)	22 (14.47)	38 (25.0)	44 (28.95)	39 (25.66)	1.441	1.222
6.	Job Security	1 (0.65)	16 (10.52)	17 (11.18)	54 (35.33	64 (42.12)	0.921	1.007
7.	Mentoring	2 (1.32)	25 (16.45)	43 (28.29)	34 (22.37)	48 (31.58)	1.322	1.149
8.	Library facility	5 (3.29)	35 (23.03)	55 (36.18)	35 (23.03)	22 (14.47)	1.776	1.062
9.	Clerical Assistance	9 (5.92)	29 (19.08)	49 (32.24)	29 (19.08)	36 (23.68)	1.586	1.334
10.	Team work	8 (5.26)	39 (25.66)	43 (28.29)	34 (22.37)	28 (18.42)	1.773	1.176
11.	Achievement	1 (0.65)	7 (4.61)	32 (21.05)	57 (37.5)	55 (36.18)	0.954	0.916
12.	Recognition	4 (2.63)	4 (2.63)	23 (15.13)	50 (32.89)	71 (46.71)	0.796	0.992
13.	Advancement	3 (1.97)	10 (6.58)	47 (30.92)	48 (31.58)	44 (28.95)	1.184	1.045
14.	Work itself	-	2 (1.31)	7 (4.61)	56 (36.84)	87 (57.24)	0.482	0.681
15.	Professional Growth	-	7 (4.61)	23 (15.13)	59 (38.81)	63 (41.45)	0.829	0.852
16.	Responsibility	2 (1.31)	8 (5.26)	25 (16.45)	61 (40.13)	56 (36.84)	0.914	0.969
17.	Creativity	7 (4.61)	5 (3.29)	24 (15.79)	44 (28.95)	72 (47.37)	0.875	1.106
18.	Involvement	-	12 (7.89)	18 (11.84)	50 (32.89)	72 (47.37)	0.789	0.953
19.	Research work	3 (1.97)	12 (7.89)	34 (22.37)	48 (31.58)	55 (36.18)	1.079	1.039
20.	Status	2 (1.31)	2 (1.3)	11 (7.24)	36 (23.68)	101 (66.45)	0.401	0.908

Source: Field Survey

V.H.G. = Very High Gap, H.G. = High Gap, M.G. = Moderate Gap, L.G. = Low Gap, N.G. = No Gap

The overall mean value and S. D. of gap in specific job satisfaction, presented in table – 3.9. It reveals that the gap in satisfaction is higher for Library facilities, Teamwork,

Clerical assistance, University policy and administration, Inter personnel relation, Mentoring, and Research work. Thus, these are the areas, which need more attention to reduce dissatisfaction of the teacher respondents in their job. Since our respondents are university teachers, the factors like Involvement, Achievement, recognition for good works, Work itself, and Responsibility have obviously the lowest possible gap in satisfaction.

Designation - Wise Analysis

The mean values of gap in specific job satisfaction presented based on the cadre of the respondents is shown in table-3.10. So far as the higher gap in satisfaction is concerned, the Professor respondents are worried for Library facilities, University policy and administration, Clerical assistance, Teamwork, and Working condition. For the Associate Professor respondents the maximum gap is for working condition, Library facilities, Teamwork, Clerical assistance, Mentoring, Inter personal relations, Advancement or promotion. In case of the Assistant Professor respondents the higher gap is indicated for Teamwork, Library facility, University policy and administration, Clerical assistance, Achievement and Research work.

Table-3.10

Designation - Wise Analysis of Gap in Job Satisfaction

Sl. No.	Various aspects Job and Job Environment	Designation of the Respondents			
		Assistant Professor	Associate Professor	Professor	Overall Mean
1.	University policy and administration	1.217	1.298	1.622	1.361
2.	Supervision	1.000	1.277	0.889	1.052
3.	Inter personal relations	1.100	1.532	1.000	1.203
4.	Pay	0.617	0.830	0.444	0.632
5.	Working conditions	1.050	2.000	1.378	1.441
6.	Job security	1.117	1.000	0.578	0.921
7.	Mentoring	1.183	1.681	1.133	1.322
8.	Library facility	1.617	1.915	1.844	1.776
9.	Clerical assistance	1.400	1.702	1.711	1.586
10.	Teamwork	1.750	1.915	1.644	1.776

11.	Achievement	1.267	1.021	0.467	0.954
12.	Recognition	0.750	0.915	0.733	0.796
13.	Advancement	1.050	1.362	1.178	1.184
14.	Work itself	0.433	0.489	0.533	0.483
15.	Professional growth	0.817	0.681	1.000	0.829
16.	Responsibility	0.917	1.085	0.733	0.914
17.	Creativity	0.683	0.979	1.022	0.875
18.	Involvement	0.750	0.872	0.756	0.789
19.	Research work	1.150	1.191	0.867	1.079
20.	Status	0.350	0.489	0.378	0.401

Source: Field Survey

NAAC Status - Wise Classification

The analysis of the data from the angle of respondents employing university's NAAC status presented in the table - 3.11.It reveals that, respondents of five star universities indicated higher gap for Library facility, Teamwork, Clerical assistance, Mentoring, University Policy and administration. The least gap is mentioned for Work itself, Recognition, Job security, Responsibility, Status, Pay and other benefits.

Table - 3.11

NAAC Status – Wise Analysis of Gap in Job Satisfaction

Sl. No.	Facets of Job and Job Environment	NAAC Status			
		***** 5 Star	**** 4 Star	*** 3 Star	Overall Mean
1.	University policy and administration	1.317	1.338	1.750	1.361
2.	Supervision	0.921	1.195	0.833	1.052
3.	Inter personal relations	1.127	1.286	1.083	1.203
4.	Pay	0.460	0.740	0.833	0.632
5.	Working conditions	1.238	1.584	1.583	1.441
6.	Job security	0.794	1.065	0.667	0.921
7.	Mentoring	1.349	1.299	1.333	1.322
8.	Library facility	2.000	1.636	1.500	1.776
9.	Clerical assistance	1.444	1.675	1.750	1.586
10.	Team Work	1.937	1.714	1.250	1.77

11.	Achievement	0.905	0.935	1.333	0.954
12.	Recognition	0.714	0.779	1.333	0.796
13.	Advancement	0.984	1.286	1.583	1.184
14.	Work itself	0.556	0.442	0.333	0.48
15.	Professional growth	0.905	0.805	0.583	0.829
16.	Responsibility	0.794	1.091	0.417	0.914
17.	Creativity	0.905	0.792	1.250	0.875
18.	Involvement	0.794	0.701	1.333	0.789
19.	Research work	1.079	1.026	1.417	1.079
20.	Status	0.413	0.429	0.167	0.401

Source: Field Survey

The employees of four star universities show their dissatisfaction by higher gaps for Clerical assistance, Library facilities, Working conditions, Inter-personal relation, while lower gaps for Status, Work itself, Professional growth, Involvement and Pay.

Three star employees have reported a higher gap in satisfaction for University policy and administration, Clerical assistance, Advancement, Library facility, Research work, Working conditions, Achievement, Recognition for good works. The lowest gap is shown by three star university employees for Status, work -itself.

Thus it can be concluded that all the respondents irrespective of NAAC status, they shown higher level of gap in job satisfaction for factors like Library facility, Teamwork, Clerical assistance, Mentoring, University policy and administration. Hence management should focus more attention for these factors to remove dissatisfaction and to motivate the employees.

Job Involvement

It is considered that Job involvement is a necessary condition if an individual is to accept fully the organization demands placed upon him by his membership in organization. Lodahal and Kejnar (1965), Job involvement is considered as "the degree to which a person is identified psychologically with his work or the importance of his work in his total self image".

In order to measure and assess the degree of job involvement of the respondents 'job involvement inventory' has been used. It was orginally developed by Lodahal and Kejnar in 1965. For the purpose of scoring the items, which are in twenty in total, were cast into a Likert format with five categories of responses, viz. strongly agree (5), Agree (4), Neither agree nor disagree (3), Disagree (2) and Strongly disagree (1). Out of the twenty items seven items were negatively phrased and, thus, reverse scored. The maximum and minimum scores are 100 and 20 respectively. High score indicates high Job involvement.

To facilitate a meaningful analysis, the range of score was split into three groups as shown below.

Low Level   :   Up to 70

Moderate Level   :   71 – 80

High Level   :   80 and above

Table – 3.12

Perceived Levels of Job Involvement of the Respondents

Range of scores and degree	Designation of the respondents			Total
	Assistant Professor	Associate Professor	Professor	
Up to 70 (Low)	17 (28.3)	12 (25.5)	6 (13.3)	35 (23.0)
71 – 80 (Moderate)	36 (60.0)	27 (57.4)	27 (60.0)	90 (59.2)
80 and above (High)	7 (11.7)	8 (17.1)	12 (26.7)	27 (17.8)
Total	60 (100.0)	47 (100.0)	45 (100.0)	152 (100.0)
Mean	74.15	74.94	76.40	75.06
S.D.	6.25	5.65	6.08	6.05

Source: Field Survey

Table-3.12 shows that, of 152 respondents 59.2 per cent of them perceived that they are moderately involved in the job, whereas the respondents having low and high level of job involvement accounted for 23.0 per cent 17.8 per cent respectively. Of 60 Assistant

Professor Respondents 60.0 per cent, of 45 Professor respondents 57.4 per cent reported moderate level of job involvement. In brief, nearly 60 per cent of the university teachers perceived moderate level of Job Involvement (mean 75.06 and S.D= 6.05)

Organizational Commitment

Organizational commitment has been viewed as reflecting an affective orientation towards the organization, recognition of costs associated with leaving the organization, and a moral obligation to remain with the organization. To acknowledge these differences, Meyer and Allen (1991) applied different labels to what they described as three components of commitment: affective, continuance, and normative.

Affective orientation is "the relative strength of an individual's identification with and involvement in a particular organization" (Mowday, porter and steers, 1982).

Continuance or Cost-Based commitment is "profit associated with continued participation and a cost associated with leaving" (Kanter 1968).

Normative commitment or obligation or Moral responsibility is "the committed employee considers it morally right to stay in the organization, regardless of how much status enhancement or satisfaction the firm gives him or her over the years" (Marsh and Mannari, 1977).

To measure organizational commitment of the university teachers, Allen and Meyer instrument put to use. The original scale comprises 8 items each, but in the revised scale affective commitment contains 8 items, 9 items comprises in the continuance commitment scale and 6 items in the normative commitment. To assess and measure the respondent's perception of organizational commitment, the respondents were asked to indicate their perceived degree of agreement or disagreement in respect of all the 23 items. The responses were analyzed on a five- point agree- disagree dimension, scored from strongly agree (5) to strongly disagree (1), and summed up. The possible range of scores in the affective commitment from 8 to 40, in the continuance commitment 9 to 45 and in normative commitment 6 to 30. This scale also consisted of seven negatively phrased and reverse-

scored items.   The total range of scores was divided into three categories: Low level,
Moderate level and High level.

Table - 3.13

Measurement of Organizational Commitment

Levels of Scores and Degree	Designation of the Respondents			Total
	Assistant Professor	Associate Professor	Professor	
A. Affective Commitment:				
Less than 25 (Low)	9 (15.0)	13 (27.7)	9 (20.0)	31 (20.4)
26-30 (Moderate)	30 (50.0)	24 (51.1)	18 (40.0)	72 (47.4)
31 and above (High)	21 (35.0)	10 (21.2)	18 (40.0)	49 (32.2)
Total	60 (100.0)	47 (100.0)	45 (100.0)	152 (100.0)
B. Continuance Commitment:				
Less than 25 (Low)	17 (28.3)	21 (44.7)	5 (11.1)	43 (28.3)
26-30 (Moderate)	19 (31.7)	13 (27.7)	18 (40.0)	50 (32.9)
31 and above (High)	24 (40.0)	13 (27.7)	22 (48.9)	59 (38.8)
Total	60 (100.0)	47 (100.0)	45 (100.0)	152 (100.0)
C. Normative Commitment:				
Less than 20 (Low)	12 (20.0)	8 (17.0)	8 (17.8)	28 (18.4)
20-25 (Moderate)	27 (45.0)	21 (44.7)	27 (60.0)	75 (49.3)
25 and above (High)	21 (35.0)	18 (38.3)	10 (22.2)	49 (32.3)
Total	60 (100.0)	47 (100.0)	45 (100.0)	152 (100.0)

D. Organizational Commitment:				
Up to 75(Low)	21 (35.0)	17 (36.2)	9 (20.0)	47 (30.9)
75-85 (Moderate)	22 (36.7)	25 (53.2)	21 (46.7)	68 (44.7)
85 and above (High)	17 (28.3)	5 (10.6)	15 (33.3)	37 (24.3)
Total	60 (100.0)	47 (100.0)	45 (100.0)	152 (100.0)
Mean	80.75	78.94	81.53	80.42
S.D.	7.191	6.20	8.25	7.27

Source: Field Survey

As shown in the table 3.13, of 152 respondents 47.4 per cent revealed moderate level of affective commitment. On the other hand, the respondents reporting low and high levels of affective commitment constituted 20.4 per cent and 32.3 per cent respectively. Of 45 Professor Respondents 40.0 per cent perceived and reported high level of affective commitment, while 35.0 per cent and 21.38 per cent of Assistant Professor and Associate Professor respondents reported high level of affective commitment.

As far as continuance commitment is concerned 38.8 per cent of the respondents indicated high level of continuance commitment, while the low and moderate level of continuance commitment account for 28.3 per cent and 32.9 per cent respectively. Professor respondents reported high level of continuance commitment.

With regard to normative commitment, of 152 respondents 49.3 per cent of them perceived moderate level. Here, 35.0 per cent of Assistant Professor and 38.3 per cent of Associate Professor Respondents have reported high level of normative commitment, while 22.2 per cent of the Professor respondents indicated high levels of normative Commitment.

In total, 44.7 percent of the respondents reported moderate level of organizational commitment and 24.3 per cent of the respondents indicated high level of organizational commitment.

96

Association of Overall Job Satisfaction and Specific Job Satisfaction

The correlation of specific job satisfaction pertaining to each of the twenty Job facets with the overall Job satisfaction of the university teachers is shown in table-3.14. Correlation ranged from 0.0139 for 'mentoring' to 0.3430 for 'research work'. The university teachers reported in respect of certain aspects of Job and Job Environment such as 'Supervision' 'Mentoring' and 'Teamwork' are not much contributed to their perception of overall job satisfaction. The factors like 'Interpersonal Relations' 'Job Security' 'Library Facility' 'Clerical Assistance' and 'Status' slightly contributed to their perception of overall Job satisfaction (The association of overall job satisfaction and specific job satisfaction are not statistically significant at 1% or 5% level of significance).

The perceived satisfaction of university teachers in respect of certain job facets like 'Pay and other benefits' 'Working conditions' 'Achievement' 'Recognition for good work' 'Promotion or advancement opportunity' 'Work it self' 'Professional growth' 'Creativity' 'Involvement' and 'Research work' significantly contributed to their perception of overall Job Satisfaction.

Based on the findings, the researcher accepted the first part of the hypothesis (H_1) - **"Over all or General Job Satisfaction of the University Teachers Significantly Associated with their Perceived Levels Specific Job Satisfaction"**

Table - 3.14

Correlation between Overall Job Satisfaction and Specific Job Satisfaction

Sl. No.	Specific Job Satisfaction	Overall J.S correlation co-efficient	Calculated 't' value	Level of Significance
1.	University policy and administration	0.1449	1.78844	5%
2.	Supervision	0.05959	0.07309	
3.	Inter personal relations	0.12010	1.48170	
4.	Pay	0.18989	2.36876	1%
5.	Working conditions	0.18989	2.36876	1%
6.	Job security	0.09782	1.20386	

7.	Mentoring	0.01392	0.17045	
8.	Library facility	0.04966	0.06089	
9.	Clerical assistance	0.13046	1.61159	
10.	Team work	0.01784	0.02185	
11.	Achievement	0.32820	4.25537	1%
12.	Recognition	0.15844	1.96533	5%
13.	Advancement	0.27590	3.51556	1%
14.	Work itself	0.23313	2.93615	1%
15.	Professional growth	0.23911	3.01604	1%
16.	Responsibility	0.21864	2.22828	1%
17.	Creativity	0.15973	1.98172	1%
18.	Involvement	0.15472	1.91808	1%
19.	Research work	0.34302	4.47241	1%
20.	Status	0.12983	1.60366	

Source: Field Survey

Table - 3.15

Inter-Correlation among Major Job Related Attitudes

Sl. No.	Job Related Attitudes	Mean	S.D	Correlation		Calculated 't' value	Level of Significance
				1	2		
1	Overall - Job Satisfaction	72.4	6.41				1%
2.	Job Involvement	75.1	6.05	0.55		8.065	5%
3.	Organizational Commitment	80.6	7.37	0.13	0.27	1.605 3.434	1%

Table-3.15 shows the mean value, standard deviation value, and inter- correlation's among the major job related attitudes. There exists a positive relationship between the university teachers perception of overall job satisfaction and job involvement(r=.55); Overall job Satisfaction and Organizational Commitment(r=.13); and their perception of Job involvement and Organizational Commitment (r=.27). The calculated't' value higher than the table value (at 1% level of significance 2.326 and 5 % level of significance 1.645).

In the light of these findings, it is accepted the second hypothesis (H_2) - **"there exists a positive relationship between job satisfaction and job involvement; between job satisfaction and organizational commitment; and between job involvement and organizational commitment"**

Reference

1. Brayfield, A.H., and Rothe, H.F., (1951), "An Index of Job Satisfaction," Journal of Applied Psychology, Vol. 35, pp. 307-311.

2. H. Frederick Herzberg, et.al., (1957), "Job Attitudes: Review of Research and Opinion," Psychological service of Pittubergh.

3. Lodahal, T. and Kejner, M., (1965), "The Definition and Measurement of Job Involvement," Journal of Applied Psychology, Vol. 49, pp. 24-33.

4. Meyer, J.P. and Allen, N.J., (1991), "A three-Component Conceptualization of Organizational Commitment," Human Resource Management Review, Vol. 1, pp. 61-89.

5. Mowday, R.T., Porter, L.W., and Steers, R., (1982), "Organizational Linkages: The Psychology of Commitment, Absenteeism, and Turnover," San Diego, CA: Academic Press.

6. Kanter, R.M., (1968), "Commitment and Social Organization: A Study of Commitment Mechanisms in Utopian Communities," American Sociological Review, Vol. 33, pp. 499-517.

7. Marsh, R.M., and Mannari, H. (1977), "Organizational Commitment and Turnover: A predictive study," Administrative Service Quarterly, Vol. 22, pp. 55-57.

CHAPTER - IV

JOB ATTITUDES: KEY DETERMINANTS

This chapter identifies and determines the major organizational, demographic, and career-related factors mainly responsible for shaping and reshaping the job attitudes of the University teachers covered by this study. The main organizational variables considered for a detailed analysis include certain characteristics of the universities such as NAAC status, age of the university, size of the university based on the total number of teaching staff, and the enrolment of students.

Demographic characteristics were the socio-economic aspects of the university teachers such as age, sex, marital status, monthly income, family structure, family size, house hold earner status, and the distance from dwelling place to work place.

Finally, the researcher considered certain variables pertaining to the career profile of the university teachers such as, designation of the respondents, work experience, workload per week (direct class room teaching hours per week), and the status of doctoral research work.

NAAC Status of the Universities and Job Attitudes

Table – 4.1, presents the relationship between the NAAC status of the respondents employing universities and their perceived level of job attitudes. Among those reported high level of overall job satisfaction, more than 91.0 per cent of the university teachers were employed in five star universities. On the other hand, 53.0 per cent experiencing low level of overall job satisfaction belonged to the four star universities. Two-way classifications of data were made to test the association between the NAAC status of the universities and general job satisfaction perceived by the university teachers. The calculated chi-square value (43.7422) was found to be greater than the table value (18.465) at .001 per cent probability level. Therefore it could be inferred that NAAC status of respondents employing universities and the overall Job satisfaction of the university teachers significantly associated.

Table – 4.1
NAAC Status of the Universities and Job Attitudes

Job Attitudes	NAAC Status			Total (N=152)	Chi-square χ^2
	***** (5 star) (n_1=95)	**** (4 star) (n_2 = 45)	*** (3 star) (n_3 =12)		
A. General Job Satisfaction:					
Low	15 (29.4)	27 (53.0)	9 (17.6)	51 (100.0)	
Moderate	35 (67.3)	15 (28.8)	2 (3.9)	52 (100.0)	43.742
High	45 (91.8)	3 (6.1)	1 (2.1)	49 (100.0)	
B. Job Involvement:					
Low	10 (28.6)	17 (48.6)	8 (28.9)	35 (100.0)	
Moderate	62 (68.9)	25 (27.8)	3 (3.3)	90 (100.0)	29.628
High	23 (85.2)	3 (11.1)	1 (3.7)	27 (100.0)	
C. Organizational Commitment					
Low	12 (25.5)	26 (55.3)	9 (19.2)	47 (100.0)	
Moderate	58 (85.3)	8 (11.8)	2 (2.9)	68 (100.0)	44.807
High	25 (67.6)	11 (29.7)	1 (2.7)	37 (100.0)	

Source: Field Survey

A similar trend could also be noticed with regard to the perception of job involvement. 85.2 per cent of the university teachers experiencing high degree of job involvement were employed in five star universities. Of 90 respondents perceiving moderate level of job involvement, 68.9 per cent of the respondents were work in those universities having four star NAAC status. From this analysis it follows that perceived degree of job involvement of university teachers was influenced by the NAAC status of the university. (Calculated Chi-square value was 29.6282, which is greater than table value at .001 per cent level of significance).

Finally, with regard to the perceived degree of organizational commitment, 67.6 per cent of the university teachers reported high degrees of organizational commitment were in the five star universities. Further 85.3 per cent of the respondents working in the five-star universities reported moderate level of organizational commitment. From this analysis, it is clear that the NAAC status of the respondents employing universities and their perceived levels of organizational commitment are associated. (χ^2 = 44.8072 at 0.01 per cent level of significance

Number of Teaching Faculty in the University and Job Attitudes

The relevant data and information in respect of the number of teaching faculty in the university and their perception of job attitudes are shown in table-4.2. 74.5 per cent of the university teachers reporting low degree of general job satisfaction belonged to those universities employing less than 300 teaching staff members, whereas 71.4 per cent perceiving high level of overall job satisfaction were employed in those universities having more than 300 teaching staff members. This trend indicates that the size of the teaching staff members in the university and their perceived levels of overall job satisfaction are associated (χ^2 = 23.2181, table value 13.815 at 0.001 percent for 2 degree of freedom).

In contrast, more than 74.0 per cent of the university teachers reporting high degree of job involvement were employed in those universities having fewer than 300 teaching staff member. On the other hand 65.7 per cent of the respondents experiencing low level of job involvement belonged to those universities having greater than 300 teaching staff member (χ^2 = 12.005 at 1% level of significance).

Table – 4.2

Number of Teaching Faculty in the University and Job Attitudes

Job Attitudes	Number of Teaching Faculty		Total (N=152)	Chi-square χ^2
	Below 300 (n_1= 85)	Above 300 (n_2 = 67)		
A. General Job Satisfaction:				
Low	38 (74.5)	13 (25.5)	51 (100.0)	
Moderate	33 (63.5)	19 (36.5)	52 (100.0)	23.218
High	14 (28.6)	35 (71.4)	49 (100.0)	
B. Job Involvement:				
Low	12 (34.3)	23 (65.7)	35 (100.0)	
Moderate	52 (57.8)	38 (42.2)	90 (100.0)	12.005
High	20 (74.1)	07 (25.9)	27 (100.0)	
C. Organizational Commitment:				
Low	15 (31.9)	32 (68.1)	47 (100.0)	
Moderate	38 (55.9)	30 (44.1)	68 (100.0)	25.011
High	32 (86.5)	5 (13.5)	37 (100.0)	

Source: Field Survey

Similarly, 68.1 per cent of the respondents perceived and reported low degree of organizational commitment represented those universities employing more than 300 teaching staff members. Whereas, out of 37 respondents perceiving high level of organizational commitment, 86.5 per cent were work for those university having less 300 teaching staff members. Thus, the size of the teaching staff members in the university influence the perception of organizational commitment of university teachers (χ^2 = 25.0119 significance at 0.001 per cent)

Age of the University and Job Attitudes

The data and information pertaining to the relationship between the age of the respondents employing universities and their job attitudes are given in table – 4.3. 81.6 per cent of the respondents reported high degree of overall job satisfaction belongs to universities aged more than 30 years. On the other hand, 68.6 per cent of the university teachers experiencing low level of overall job satisfaction were employed in those universities aged less than 30 years. This trend clearly indicates that, there is an association between the age of the universities and the perception of the overall job satisfaction of the university teachers (χ^2 = 32.203 at 0.01 per cent level of significance for 2 degrees of freedom).

Similarly, out of 35 respondents 26 (74.3 per cent) represented to those universities aged less than 30 years reported low level of job involvement. On the other hand, slightly more than 70.0 percent of the respondents perceiving high degree of job involvement belonged to those universities aged more than 30 years. This trend is indicative of relationship between the age of university and the respondent's perception of Job involvement (χ^2 = 26.399 at .01 per cent level of significant for 2 degree of freedom).

68.1 per cent of the university teachers perceiving low level of organizational commitment were employed in those universities aged below 30 years whereas, 89.7 per cent and 51.4 per cent of the respondents reporting moderate and high level of organizational commitment belonged to those universities aged more than 30 years. Two-way analysis of data was made to test the significance of association these two variables. The calculated chi-square value is greater than the table value at 0.01 per cent level of significance.

Table - 4.3

Age of the Universities and Job Attitudes

Job Attitudes	Age of the Universities (in years)		Total (N=152)	Chi-square χ^2
	Below 30 (n_1= 57)	Above 30 (n_2 = 95)		
A. Overall Job Satisfaction:				
Low	35 (68.6)	16 (31.4)	51 (100.00)	
Moderate	13 (25.0)	39 (75.0)	52 (100.0)	32.203
High	9 (18.4)	40 (81.6)	49 (100.0)	
B. Job Involvement:				
Low	26 (74.3)	9 (25.7)	35 (100.0)	
Moderate	23 (25.5)	67 (74.5)	90 (100.0)	26.399
High	8 (29.6)	19 (70.4)	27 (100.0)	
C. Organizational Commitment:				
Low	32 (68.1)	15 (31.9)	47 (100.0)	
Moderate	7 (10.3)	61 (89.7)	68 (100.0)	42.195
High	18 (48.6)	19 (51.4)	37 (100.0)	

Source: Field Survey

Number of Students Enrolment and Job Attitudes

As seen in the table – 4.4, more than 61.0 per cent of the university teachers reporting high degree of overall job satisfaction belonged to those universities enrolling more than 3000 students. On the other hand, 58.8 percent perceiving low level of general job satisfaction in those universities having student enrolment is less than 3000. Hence, the size of universities based on student enrolment and the perceptions of job satisfaction among university teachers are associated. (χ^2= 8.553 at .01 per cent level of significant)

Table – 4.4

Number of Students Enrolment and Job Attitudes

Job Attitudes	Number of Students Enrolment		Total (N=152)	Chi-square χ^2
	Below 3000 (n₁= 77)	Above 3000 (n₂ = 75)		
A. General Job Satisfaction:				
Low	30 (58.8))	21 (41.2)	51 (100.0)	
Moderate	28 (53.8)	24 (46.2)	52 (100.0)	8.553
High	19 (38.8)	30 (61.2)	49 (100.0)	
B. Job Involvement:				
Low	12 (34.3)	23 (65.7)	35 (100.0)	
Moderate	44 (48.9)	46 (51.1)	90 (100.0)	11.810
High	21 (77.8)	6 (22.2)	27 (100.0)	
C. Organizational Commitment:				
Low	32 (68.1)	15 (31.9)	47 (100.0)	
Moderate	38 (55.9)	30 (44.1)	68 (100.0)	20.991
High	7 (18.9)	30 (81.1)	37 (100.0)	

Source: Field Survey

In contrast, 77.8 per cent perceiving high level of job involvement were employed in those universities having less than 3000 student enrolment whereas, 65.7 per cent of the university teachers reported low level of job involvement represent to those universities student enrolment was more than 3000 students. Thus, the student enrolment in the universities tends to influence the perception of job involvement of the university teachers. (χ^2 = 11.810 at .01 per cent level of significance)

As far as organizational commitment of the universities teacher is concerned, 81.1 per cent of the respondent reporting high degree of organizational commitment represented to those universities enrolling more than 3000 students, whereas 68.1 per cent perceiving low degree of organizational commitment were employed in those universities having less than 3000 students. This trend suggests that the student size in the university and the perceived levels of organizational commitment of the teachers are significantly associated (χ^2 = 20.991 at 0.01 per cent level of significance)

Age of the Respondents and Job Attitude

As far as age of the respondents and their perceived levels of job attitude is concerned, table – 4.5 reveals that 67.3 per cent of the university teachers reporting high degree of overall job satisfaction were above the age of 42 years. On the other hand, 66.7 per cent of the university teachers perceiving low level of overall job satisfaction were below the age of 42 years. From this it is clear that there is an association between the age of the university and their perceived level of overall job satisfaction. (The chi-square value statistically significant at 1% level)

Similarly, more than 85.0 per cent of the university teachers reporting high level of job involvement were more than 42 years old, whereas 71.4 per cent of the university teachers reported low degree of job involvement were below the age of 42 years. Thus, the age group of the university teachers tends to influence their perception of job involvement. (χ^2 = 19.612 at 1% level of significance)

Table – 4.5

Age of the Respondents and Job Attitude

Job Attitudes	Age of the respondents (in years)		Total (N=152)	Chi-square χ^2
	Below 42 (n_1= 72)	Above 42 (n_2=80)		
A. General Job Satisfaction:				
Low	34 (66.7)	17 (33.3)	51 (100.0)	
Moderate	22 (42.3)	30 (57.7)	52 (100.0)	12.413
High	16 (32.7)	33 (67.3)	49 (100.0)	
B. Job Involvement:				
Low	25 (71.4)	10 (28.6)	35 (100.0)	19.612

107

Moderate	43 (47.8)	47 (52.2)	90 (100.0)	
High	4 (14.8)	23 (85.2)	27 (100.0)	
C. Organizational Commitment:				
Low	35 (74.5)	12 (25.5)	47 (100.0)	
Moderate	23 (33.8)	45 (66.2)	68 (100.0)	20.245
High	14 (37.8)	23 (62.2)	37 (100.0)	

Source: Field Survey

Further, among those university teachers reported high degree of organizational commitment, 62.2 per cent are in the age group of above 42 years. On the other hand 74.5 per cent of the university teachers perceived low level of organizational commitment were below age of 42 years. Therefore, the age of the university teachers tends to influence their perception of organizational commitment. In short, based on chi-square test (at 1% level of significance for 2 degree of freedom) it could be inferred that age of the respondents and their organization commitment is associated.

Sex of the Respondents and Job Attitudes

Table – 4.6, reveals that the data and information relating to the association between the sex of the respondents and their perceived level of job attitudes. It is interesting to observe that among those university teachers perceiving high level of overall job satisfaction, as high as nearly 94.0 per cent were male, whereas 52.9 per cent of the teachers reported low levels of overall job satisfaction were female. The chi- square (χ^2) results revealed the significant association between the sex of the respondents and perceived level of job satisfaction.

It should be noted that, out of 35 respondents perceiving low level of job involvement only 6 (17.1 per cent) were women teachers. On the other hand 74.0 per cent of the university teachers indicating high level of job involvement were female respondents. From this it is clear that, there is an association between sex of the respondents and perceived level of job involvement. ($\chi^2 = 51.545$ significance at 0.01 per cent)

108

Further, among those university teachers reporting high degree of organizational commitment, 91.9 percent were male and more than 61.0 percent perceiving low degree of organizational commitment were female. Hence, sex of the respondents and their perception of organizational commitment are closely related (χ^2 = 60.987 at 1% level of significance).

In short, it could be inferred that most of the university teachers perceiving high degree of general job satisfaction and organizational commitment were male employees, and greater proportion of the university teachers reporting high level of job involvement were female respondents.

Table – 4.6
Sex of the Respondents and Job Attitudes

Job Attitudes	Sex of the Respondents		Total (N=152)	Chi-square χ^2
	Male (n$_1$= 118)	Female (n$_2$ = 34)		
A. General Job Satisfaction				
Low	24 (47.1)	27 (52.9)	51 (100.0)	
Moderate	48 (92.3)	4 (7.7)	52 (100.0)	41.348
High	46 (93.9)	3 (6.1)	49 (100.0)	
B. Job Involvement:				
Low	29 (82.9)	6 (17.1)	35 (100.0)	
Moderate	82 (91.1)	8 (8.9)	90 (100.0)	51.545
High	7 (26.0)	20 (74.0)	27 (100.0)	
C. Organizational Commitment:				
Low	18 (38.3)	29 (61.7)	47 (100.0)	
Moderate	66 (97.1)	2 (2.9)	68 (100.0)	60.987
High	34 (91.9)	3 (8.1)	37 (100.0)	

Source: Filed Survey

Marital Status and Job Attitudes

The relevant data and information in respect of marital status of the respondents and their perception of job attitudes are shown in table-4.7. Among those university teachers experiencing high degree of overall job satisfaction, 95.9 per cent were married. On the other hand, only 4.1 percent of the university teachers reporting high degree of overall job satisfaction were unmarried. From this analysis it follows that the marital status of the university teachers tends to influence their perception of overall job satisfaction ($\chi^2 = 9.924$ significant at 1% level)

Table – 4.7

Marital Status and Job Attitudes

Job Attitudes	Marital Status		Total (N=152)	Chi-square χ^2
	Married ($n_1= 38$)	Single ($n_2 = 14$)		
A. General Job Satisfaction:				
Low	41 (80.4)	10 (19.6)	51 (100.0)	
Moderate	50 (96.2)	2 (3.8)	52 (100.0)	9.924
High	47 (95.9)	2 (4.1)	49 (100.0)	
B. Job Involvement				
Low	27 (77.1)	8 (22.9)	35 (100.0)	
Moderate	86 (95.6)	4 (4.4)	90 (100.0)	10.344
High	25 (92.6)	2 (7.4)	27 (100.0)	
C. Organizational Commitment:				
Low	36 (76.6)	11 (23.4)	47 (100.0)	
Moderate	66 (97.1)	2 (2.9)	68 (100.0)	16.393
High	36 (97.3)	1 (2.7)	37 (100.0)	

Source: Field Survey

It should be noted that 92.0 to 95.0 percent of the university teachers perceiving high to moderate levels of job involvement were married. On the other hand, only 4.0 to 7.0

percent of the university teachers reported moderates to high degree of job involvement were unmarried. Therefore, it is inferred that there is an association between marital status of the respondent and their perceived levels of job involvement ($\chi^2 = 10.344$ at 1% level of significance).

A similar trend could also been observed in respect of relationship between marital status of the respondents and their perception of the organizational commitment. As high as 97.3 per cent of the respondents indicating high level of organizational commitments were married respondents. In other words only 2.7 percent of the university teachers perceiving high degree of organizational commitment were unmarried. Hence, there exists an association between the marital status of the university teachers and perceived level of organizational commitment.

Total Monthly Income and Job Attitudes

With regard to relationship between total monthly income of the university teachers and their perceived levels of job attitudes, as seen in table – 4.8, 69.3 per cent of the university teachers perceiving high degree of general job satisfaction were earning income in total more than `.50,000 per month. On the other hand 75.0 per cent of them indicating low degree of overall job satisfaction possessed on average monthly income of less than `.50, 000. Hence, it is inferred that, the monthly income of the university teachers and their perception of overall job satisfaction are associated. ($\chi^2 = 45.043$ at 1% level of significance)

74.4 percent of the university teachers perceiving moderate level of job involvement had an average monthly income more than 50,000. On the other hand, 68.6 per cent (24 out of 35) of the university teachers perceived low level of job involvement earned less than `50,000 per month. This trend indicates that there is an association between the total monthly income and their perception of job involvement ($\chi^2 = 20.072$ at 1% level of significance).

Table – 4.8

Total Monthly Income and Job Attitudes

Job Attitudes	Total Monthly Income (In `.)		Total (N=152)	Chi-square χ^2
	Less than 50,000 (n_1= 59)	More than 50,000 (n_2 = 93)		
A. General Job satisfaction:				
Low	38 (75.0)	13 (25.0)	51 (100.0)	
Moderate	6 (11.5)	46 (88.5)	52 (100.0)	45.043
High	15 (30.6)	34 (69.3)	49 (100.0)	
B. Job Involvement:				
Low	24 (68.6)	11 (31.4)	35 (100.0)	
Moderate	23 (25.6)	67 (74.4)	90 (100.0)	20.072
High	12 (44.4)	15 (55.6)	27 (100.0)	
C. Organizational Commitment:				
Low	32 (68.1)	15 (31.9)	47 (100.0)	
Moderate	15 (22.1)	53 (77.9)	68 (100.0)	25.629
High	12 (32.4)	25 (67.6)	37 (100.0)	

Source: Field Survey

It should be noted that 67.0 to 78.0 per cent of the university teachers indicating high to moderate level organizational commitment earned, on an average, a total monthly income of more than `50,000. In contrast, as high as 68.0 per cent of them perceiving low level of organizational commitment earned less than ` 50,000 per month. From this it follows that the average monthly income of the university teachers tends to influence their perceived levels of organizational commitment (χ^2 = 25.629 greater than the table value at 1% level of significance)

112

Family Structure of the Respondents and their Job Attitudes:

The data and information pertaining to the relationship between the family structure of the university teacher and their perceived levels of job attitudes are presented in table – 4.9. Among those university teachers perceiving high degree of job satisfaction, 98.0 per cent belonged to nuclear families. On the other hand only 2.0 per cent of university teachers indicating high degree of job satisfaction live in the extended families. Thus, the type of family structure of the university teacher and their perception of overall job satisfaction are associated (χ^2 = 18.248 at 1% level of significance).

Of the 90 university teachers reporting moderate level of job involvement, 93.3 percent belonged to nuclear families, whereas 88.9 percent indicating high level of job involvement also belongs to nuclear families. From this analysis, it follows that the type of family structure of the university teachers and their perception of job involvement are associated (χ^2 = 8.774 at 1% level of significance).

As far as the relationship between organizational commitment and family structure of the university teachers is concerned, greater proportions say, 94.6 per cent of the university teachers perceiving high degree of organizational commitment belonged to the nuclear families. Only 5.4 per cent of the respondents reported high degree of organizational commitment belongs to the extended families. Hence, the relationship between the family structure and organizational commitment of the university teachers are statistically significant at 1% level.

Table - 4.9

Family Structure of the Respondents and their Job Attitudes

Job Attitudes	Family Structure		Total (N=152)	Chi-square χ^2
	Nuclear (n_1= 134)	Extended (n_2 = 18)		
A. General Job Satisfaction:				
Low	37 (72.5)	14 (27.5)	51 (100.0)	18.248
Moderate	49 (94.2)	3 (5.8)	52 (100.0)	

113

High	48 (98.0)	1 (2.0)	49 (100.0)	
B. Job Involvement: Low	26 (74.3)	9 (25.7)	35 (100.0)	
Moderate	84 (93.3)	6 (6.7)	90 (100.0)	8.774
High	24 (88.9)	3 (11.1)	27 (100.0)	
C. Organizational Commitment: Low	35 (74.5)	12 (25.5)	47 (100.0)	
Moderate	64 (94.1)	4 (5.9)	68 (100.0)	12.219
High	35 (94.6)	2 (5.4)	37 (100.0)	

Source: Field Survey

Household Earners status and Job Attitudes

With regard to the relationship between the household earner status of the university teachers and their perceived levels of job attitudes are presented in the table- 4.10. It is clear that 64.7 per cent of the university teachers perceiving low level of general job satisfaction belonged to more than one earner household. On the other hand, 87.8 per cent of them revealing high degree of general job satisfaction represented single earner household. It could be inferred that there is an association between household earner status of the university teachers and their perceived level of overall job satisfaction (χ^2= 36.092 at 1% level of significance).

114

Table – 4.10

Household Earners Status and Job Attitudes

Job Attitudes	Household Earner Status		Total (N=152)	Chi-square χ^2
	Single earner (n_1= 102)	More than one earner ($n_2 = 50$)		
A. General Job Satisfaction:				
Low	18 (35.3)	33 (64.7)	51 (100.0)	
Moderate	41 (78.9)	11 (21.1)	52 (100.0)	36.092
High	43 (87.8)	6 (12.2)	49 (100.0)	
B. Job Involvement:				
Low	13 (37.1)	22 (62.9)	35 (100.0)	
Moderate	69 (76.7)	21 (23.3)	90 (100.0)	18.555
High	20 (74.1)	07 (26.9)	27 (100.0)	
C. Organizational Commitment:				
Low	41 (87.2)	6 (12.7)	47 (100.0)	
Moderate	54 (79.4)	14 (20.6)	68 (100.0)	52.211
High	7 (18.9)	30 (81.1)	37 (100.0)	

Source: Field Survey

It could be seen that, 62.9 per cent of the university teachers indicating low level of job involvement belonged to more than one earner hose hold, while 74.1 percent of them reporting high level of job involvement had single earner household status. Hence, the household earner status and their perception of job involvement reflect a close relationship.

In contrast, among those university teachers reporting high degree of organizational commitment, more than 81.0 per cent belonged to more than one earner household. On the other hand, 87.2 per cent of the university teachers indicating low level of organizational commitment had single earner household status. This trend suggests that there is relationship between the household earners status of the university teachers and the perception of organizational commitment.

Family Size of the Respondents and Job Attitudes

Table - 4.11 shows that the relationship between the family size of the university teachers and their perceived level of job attitudes. Among those university teachers perceiving high level of general job satisfaction, 57.1 per cent had a family size of less than four members. On the other hand, 88.2 per cent of the university teachers indicating low level of overall job satisfaction belonged to those families having more than four members. This trend indicates that family size of the university teacher tend to influence overall job satisfaction (χ^2 = 30.937 at 1% level of significance).

As far as job involvement is concerned, 77.1 per cent of the university teachers reporting low degree of job involvement had a family size of more than four members. On the other hand, 81.5 per cent of university teachers perceiving high level of job involvement belonged to those families having less than four members. Therefore it could be inferred that, there exists relationship between the family size of the university teachers and their perception of job involvement (χ^2 = 18.555 at 1% level of significance).

Table – 4.11

Family Size of the Respondents and Job Attitudes

Job Attitudes	Family Size (in number)		Total (N=152)	Chi-square χ^2
	Less than 4 (n_1= 46)	More than 4 (n_2 = 106)		
A. General Job Satisfaction:				
Low	6 (11.8)	45 (88.2)	51 (100.0)	30.937
Moderate	12 (23.1)	40 (76.9)	52 (100.0)	

High	28 (57.1)	21 (42.9)	49 (100.0)	
B. Job Involvement:				
Low	8 (22.9)	27 (77.1)	35 (100.0)	
Moderate	16 (17.8)	74 (82.2)	90 (100.0)	18.555
High	22 (81.5)	5 (18.5)	27 (100.0)	
C. Organizational Commitment:				
Low	5 (10.5)	42 (89.4)	47 (100.0)	
Moderate	12 (17.6)	56 (82.4)	68 (100.0)	52.211
High	29 (78.4)	8 (21.6)	37 (100.0)	

Source: Field Survey

Lastly, 78.4 per cent of the university teachers reporting high level of organizational commitment had a family size of less than four members, while 89.4 per cent of the university teachers perceiving low level of organizational commitment belong to those families having more than four member families. Hence, it is concluded that there exists a relationship between the family size of the respondents and their perceived levels of organizational commitment. (χ^2 = 52.211 at 1% level of significance)

Distance from dwelling place to work place and Job Attitudes

With regard to the relationship between the distance from dwelling place to work place and their perceived levels of job attitudes, as seen in table – 4.12, 79.6 per cent of the university teachers perceiving high degree of overall job satisfaction resides with in the 5 K.M distance from their work place. On the hand, 62.7 per cent of the university teachers perceived low level of general job satisfaction resides more than 5 K.M from working place. This trend is indicative of relationship between the distance from dwelling place to work place and their perception of overall job satisfaction (χ^2 = 21.345 at 1% level of significance).

It should be noted that 70.4 per cent of the university teachers indicating high degree of job involvement reside less than 5 K.M from their work place. On the other hand, more than 65.0 per cent of the university teachers reporting low level of job involvement dwelling place is more than 5 K.M from their working place. Hence, the distance from dwelling place to work place and their perceived degree of job involvement reflect a close relationship ($\chi^2 = 8.251$ at 1% level of significant).

Finally 58.0 to 62.0 percent of the university teachers perceiving moderate to high degree of organizational commitment resides nearer to the working place (with in the 5 K.M). On the hand, 63.8 percent university teachers reporting low degree or organizational commitment reside far away from the work place (more than 5 K.M). From this analysis, it follows that the distance from dwelling place to work place of the respondents and their perceived degree of organizational commitment are associated ($\chi^2 = 7.502$ at 1% level of significance).

Table – 4.12

Distance from Dwelling Place to Work Place and Job Attitudes

Job Attitudes	Distance from Dwelling Place to Work Place (in k.m)		Total (N=152)	Chi-square χ^2
	Less than 5 (n_1= 80)	More than 5 (n_2 = 72)		
A. General Job Satisfaction:				
Low	19 (37.3)	32 (62.7)	51 (100.0)	
Moderate	22 (42.3)	30 (57.7)	52 (100.0)	21.345
High	39 (79.6)	10 (20.4)	49 (100.0)	
B. Job Involvement:				
Low	12 (34.3)	23 (65.7)	35 (100.0)	
Moderate	49 (54.4)	41 (45.5)	90 (100.0)	8.251
High	19 (70.4)	8 (29.6)	27 (100.0)	

C. Organizational Commitment:				
Low	17 (36.2)	30 (63.8)	47 (100.0)	
Moderate	40 (58.8)	28 (41.2)	68 (100.0)	7.502
High	23 (62.2)	14 (37.8)	37 (100.0)	

Source: Field Survey

Position of the Respondents and Job Attitudes

Table – 4.13 shows the relationship between the position of the respondents and their perceived levels of job attitudes. Nearly 60.0 per cent of the university teachers reported low levels of overall job satisfaction were Assistant Professor Respondents. On the other hand 34.0 to 38.0 per cent of the university teachers perceiving high to moderate levels of overall job satisfaction are Professor Respondents. From this it is clear that, there is an association between the position of the university teachers and their perceived level of overall job satisfaction. ($\chi^2 = 7.913$ at 5% level of significance)

Table – 4.13

Position of the Respondents and Job Attitudes

Job Attitudes	Positional Level of the Respondents			Total (N=152)	Chi-Square χ^2
	Professors (n_1=45)	Associate Professors (n_2 = 47)	Assistant Professor (n_3 =12)		
A. General Job Satisfaction:					
Low	8 (15.7)	17 (33.3)	26 (50.9)	51 (100.0)	
Moderate	20 (38.5)	15 (28.8)	17 (32.7)	52 (100.0)	7.913
High	17 (34.7)	15 (30.6)	17 (34.7)	49 (100.0)	

119

B. Job Involvement:					
Low	6 (17.1)	12 (34.3)	17 (48.6)	35 (100.0)	
Moderate	27 (30.0)	27 (30.0)	36 (40.0)	90 (100.0)	6.012
High	12 (44.4)	8 (29.6)	7 (26.0)	27 (100.0)	
C. Organizational Commitment:					
Low	9 (19.1)	17 (36.1)	21 (44.8)	47 (100.0)	
Moderate	21 (30.9)	25 (36.8)	22 (32.3)	68 (100.0)	9.652
High	15 (40.5)	5 (13.5)	17 (46.0)	37 (100.0)	

Source: Field Survey

As far as the perceived level of job involvement of the university teachers and their position of the respondent is concerned, 44.4 per cent of the university teachers indicating high degree of job involvement are Professor Respondents. On the other hand, 48.6 per cent of the university teachers perceived low level of job involvement are Lecture respondents. Hence, it is concluded that the position of the university teachers and their perceived level of job involvement are associated. ($\chi^2 = 6.012$ at 5% level of significance)

Similarly, 30.0 to 40.0 per cent of the university teachers reported moderate to high degree of organizational commitment are Professor Respondents. On the other hand, 44.8 per cent of the university teachers perceived low level of organizational commitment are Assistant Professor Respondents. From this it is clear that there is an association between position of the respondents and their perceived level of organizational commitment. ($\chi^2 = 9.652$ at 1% level of significance)

Table 4.14

Work Experience of the Respondents and their Job Attitudes

Job Attitudes	Work Experience (in years)		Total (N=152)	Chi-square χ^2
	Below 15 (n_1= 77)	Above 15 (n_2 = 75)		
A. Overall Job Satisfaction:				
Low	35 (68.6)	16 (31.4)	51 (100.00)	
Moderate	23 (44.2)	29 (55.8)	52 (100.0)	10.215
High	19 (38.7)	30 (61.2)	49 (100.0)	
B. Job Involvement:				
Low	26 (74.3)	9 (25.7)	35 (100.0)	
Moderate	31 (34.4)	59 (65.6)	90 (100.0)	14.537
High	7 (25.9)	20 (74.1)	27 (100.0)	
C. Organizational Commitment:				
Low	31 (66.0)	16 (34.0)	47 (100.0)	
Moderate	32 (47.1)	36 (52.9)	68 (100.0)	7.186
High	14 (37.8)	23 (62.2)	37 (100.0)	

Source: Field Survey

An attempt was made to understand the relationship between the work experience of the university teachers and their perceived levels of job attitudes. As seen in table – 4.14, among those university teachers reporting low degree of overall job satisfaction 68.6 per cent of them had less than fifteen years of job experience. On the contrary, 61.2 per cent of them revealing high degree of general job satisfaction possessed more than fifteen years of experience. This reflects the association between the work experience of the respondents and their perception of overall job satisfaction. (χ^2 = 10.215 at 1.0 per cent level of significance)

Similar trend could also see in respect of the work experience and its relationship to the perceived levels of job involvement. Among those perceiving low degree of job involvement, a greater proportion of 74.3 per cent having less than fifteen years of teaching and research experience. On the other hand 74.1 of them indicating high degree of job involvement had more than fifteen years of experience. The two-way classification of data was made for chi-square test, the results reveals that there is a relationship between job experiences of the respondents and degree of job involvement. ($\chi^2 = 14.537$ at 1% level of significance)

Identical findings were also observed in respect of organizational commitment. Among those university teachers perceived low level of organizational commitment, 66.0 per cent had less than fifteen years of experience. On the other hand, 52.9 per cent of their perceiving high degree of organizational commitment possessed more than fifteen years of experience. Hence, it is concluded that work experience and organizational commitment are associated. ($\chi^2 = 7.186$ at 1% level of significance)

Table - 4.15

Work Load and Job Attitudes

Job Attitudes	Work Load Per Week (in hours)		Total (N=152)	Chi-square χ^2
	Below 12 (n_1= 82)	Above 12 (n_2 = 70)		
A. Overall Job Satisfaction:				
Low	35 (68.6)	16 (31.4)	51 (100.00)	
Moderate	38 (73.1)	14 (26.9)	52 (100.0)	37.051
High	9 (18.4)	40 (81.6)	49 (100.0)	
B. Job Involvement:				
Low	9 (25.7)	26 (74.3	35 (100.0)	
Moderate	52 (57.8)	38 (42.2)	90 (100.0)	17.932
High	21 (77.8)	6 (22.2)	27 (100.0)	

C. **Organizational Commitment:**				
Low	29 (61.7)	18 (38.3)	47 (100.0)	
Moderate	31 (45.6)	37 (54.4)	68 (100.0)	3.502
High	22 (59.5)	15 (40.5)	37 (100.0)	

Source: Field Survey

The data and information pertaining to the relationship between workload per week (direct classroom teaching) and their perception of the job attitudes are given in table – 4.15. Among those universities, teaching reporting low level of job satisfaction, as high as 68.6 percent of them engaging less than twelve hours of direct classroom teaching. On the other hand, 81.6 percent of the perceived high degree of overall job satisfaction is engaging more than twelve hours of direct classroom teaching per week. This trend indicates there is an association between the number of hours of direct classroom teaching and job satisfaction of the university teachers. (χ^2 = 37.051, significance at 1 per cent level)

In contrast, more than 74.0 per cent of the university teachers revealing low level of job involvement accounted for those having work load more than 12 hours per week. On the other hand, 77.8 per cent reveling high degree of job involvement engaging less than 12 hours of direct class room teaching per week. Thus there exists a close association between the workload (direct classroom teaching per week) and their perception of job involvement. (χ^2 = test shows significance relations at 1 per cent level)

As far as work load and perception of organizational commitment of the university teachers are concerned, 61.7 per cent of the university teachers reporting low level of organizational commitment accounted for those engaging less then twelve hours of direct class room teaching. However, there existed only marginal variations in the perception of moderate to high level of organizational commitment of those university teachers engaging more than 12 hours and less than 12 hours of teaching work. (χ^2 =3.502 significance at .05 per cent level)

Table - 4.16

Status of Doctoral Research Work and Job Attitudes

Job Attitudes	Status of Doctoral Research Work		Total (N=152)	Chi-square χ^2
	Ph.D. holders (n_1=130)	Non Ph.D. holders (n_2 = 22)		
A. Overall Job Satisfaction:				
Low	33 (64.7)	18 (35.3)	51 (100.0)	
Moderate	50 (96.2)	2 (3.8)	52 (100.0)	26.878
High	47 (96.0)	2 (4.0)	49 (100.0)	
B. Job Involvement:				
Low	15 (42.9)	20 (57.1)	35 (100.0)	
Moderate	89 (98.9)	1 (1.1)	90 (100.0)	66.989
High	26 (96.3)	1 (3.7)	27 (100.0)	
C. Organizational Commitment:				
Low	32 (68.1)	15 (31.9)	47 (100.0)	
Moderate	63 (92.4)	5 (7.3)	68 (100.0)	16.793
High	35 (94.6)	2 (5.4)	37 (100.0)	

Source: Field Survey

As seen in the above table – 4.16, among those reported high level of general job satisfaction 96.0 per cent of them possessed their doctoral degree. Only 4.0 percent of the respondent's revealed high degrees of overall job satisfaction are non-Ph.D. degree holders. Whereas in the low levels of job satisfaction 64.7 per cent are doctoral degree holder and rest is non-doctoral degree holder. However, there is moderately relationship between status of the doctoral research work of the respondents and their perceived levels of overall job satisfaction.

With regard to status of doctoral research work of the university teachers and their perceived levels of job involvement is concerned, 57.1 per cent of the respondents reporting low level of job involvement did not possessed doctoral degree. On the other hand, as high as 96.3 percent of the teachers reveling high degree of job involvement are Ph.D. degrees holders. Hence, there is an association between the status of the doctoral research work and their perceived degree of job involvement (χ^2 = 66.989 at 1percent level of significance).

Finally, among those reported high degree of organizational commitment more than 94.0 per cent possessed doctoral degree. On the other hand, low levels of organization commitment reported by doctorates and non-doctorates are 68.1 per cent and 31.9 per cent respectively. It is obvious that, there is an association between status of the doctoral research work and perceived degree of organizational commitment.

In summary, majority of the university teachers reported high levels of overall job satisfaction, job involvement, and organizational commitment belonged to five stars NAAC accredited universities; those universities aged more than 30 years. A significant number of university teachers perceiving high degree of job satisfaction were employed in those universities having more than 300 teaching faculty members. Whereas, most of them experiencing high levels of job involvement and organizational commitment were found in those universities employing less than 300 teaching faculty members. Similarly, most of the respondents reporting high degree of job satisfaction and organizational commitment were identified in those universities enrolling more than 3000 students. While, majority of them experiencing high degree of job involvement were found in those university enrolled less than 3000 students.

As far as the socio- economic characteristics of the university teachers are concerned, the majority of the University teachers reporting high degree of job satisfaction, job involvement, and organizational commitment were above the age of 42 years, were enjoying married life, had an monthly income of more than `. 25,000, belongs to nuclear families, having a smaller family of fewer than 4 members and distance from dwelling place to work place is less than 5 K.M. Most of them experiencing a high level of overall job satisfaction and organizational commitment were male employees. Whereas, a greater proportion of the women University teachers reporting high level of job involvement. Similarly, a sizable proportion of them reporting a high degree of job satisfaction and job involvement belonged to the single-earner household. While, there is a significant number of them reporting high level of organizational commitment represented more than one-earner household.

With regard to the career-related factors, a greater proportion of the University teachers perceiving high degree of job satisfaction, job involvement and organizational commitment had a job experience of more than 15 years, having Ph.D. degree qualification. Similarly, about one-half of the University teachers indicating high degree of job satisfaction and job involvement were professor respondents. Fifty per cent of the Assistant Professor Respondents reported high degree of organizational commitment.

Finally, there exists an association between job satisfaction and number of hour of workload per week, organizational commitment and number of hours of workload per week.

Based on the result and discussions presented above, the third part of hypothesis (H3) accepted- **"Organizational, Socio-Economic and Career related factors influences to perceived levels of job attitudes of university teachers.**

CHAPTER - V

ATTITUDES OF UNIVERSITY TEACHERS TOWARDS STUDENT EVALUATION OF TEACHERS (SET)

Teachers are always evaluated. The origin of the student evaluation of teaching and teacher's self-evaluation can be traced to the time of Socrates in the West (Millman, J.1981)[1] and Panini in the East (Mookerji, 1969)[2] in about six cenury B.C., when they were gathered informally and unsystematically. Higher education in the western, developed countries has about 100 year's long and rich tradition of semi-systematic and systematic teacher evaluation by students.

Meaning

Appraisal is the process of evaluating the relative worth or ability of teacher (Assistant Professor/Associate Professor/ Professor) against pre-determined, job-related performance standards usually set by job-descriptions. Performance appraisal replaces casual assessment with formal and systematic procedures. In this process, teachers know that they are being evaluated and are being told the criteria that will be used in the course of the appraisal.

The appraisal of employees has been variously described over the years as merit rating, behavioral assessment, employee's evaluation, personnel review, progress report, self-assessment, service rating and fitness report etc.

Evaluators

Self, peers, students, administrators, parents and the public, and professional evaluators or researchers all of these actors can have an important role in the evaluation of teachers, but all are not equally suited to evaluate all aspects of teaching.

Stages of Performance Appraisal System

1. Establishing performance standards.
2. Communication of performance expectations to teachers.

3. Measurement of actual performance.

4. Comparison of actual performance with standards.

5. Discussion of the appraisal with the teacher and

6. If necessary, initiation of corrective action.

Performance Appraisal as Part of HRD

Every institution needs to ensure right number and right kind of people at the right time capable of effectively completing the task that helps the organization to achieve its educational and non-educational objective.

A current inventory of the talents can be made only through a valid appraisal process that shows those who perform well and those who cannot. In addition, performance appraisal can be put to several uses covering entire spectrum of personnel/ human resource functions in an institution, which may include.

1. Systematic effort to tone up effective teaching based on evaluation results, appropriate feedback and corrective action.

2. Input for an array of personnel decisions such as placement, transfer, promotion and rewards.

3. To identify individuals with high potential and merits.

4. To develop career planning particularly for young teaching staff

5. For diagnosing individual and orgnisational problems, and

6. To validate National Educational Test and other selection processes for the Assistant Professors.

Present System of Performance Appraisal

In Karnataka State, for the evaluation of performance, like other government organizations confidential report system is followed in government colleges and universities. A confidential report is a report on the subordinate by the immediate supervisor and cover limited range of aspects like candidate's strengths and weaknesses, major achievements and failures and information on some personality traits and behavioral aspects. The confidential report used in Karnataka government colleges and universities consists of three main sections.

128

Section I consists of particulars of the teacher (appraiser) including name, academic qualifications, date of birth, home district and district where presently employed, post occupied and grade, etc.

Section II is related to self-assessment of teacher regarding his/ her own educational achievements. It mainly includes, research project undertaken, books, articles and research papers published, number of research students awarded Ph.D degree, national and international conferences attended, extension and administrative responsibilities of the institution entrusted.

Section III refers to appraisal remark of reporting officer (principal/ Chairman) to be communicated to the higher authorities (Director/ Registrar). The principal or chairman evaluates the achievements and personality traits of the teacher in terms of his/her communicating abilities, intellectual level, teaching abilities, regularities, dedication to duties, relationship with colleagues and students. The last two columns are left for the remarks of reviewing authority and accepting authority. A negative confidential report is required to be communicated to the ratee, and if the ratee disagrees, there should be nothing of the format to that affect.

Drawbacks in the Confidential Report System

A confidential report system is usually a descriptive one and permits a lot of subjectivity.

1. Superficial Treatment

Although a free report system expects a superior to think seriously about the subordinate qualities but the principal/chairperson of the institution/ department/ Registrar of the universities are mostly busy in handling other administrative problems and might treat the appraisal work superficially, since the activity is time consuming.

2. ill- defined Criteria and Ambiguity

Criteria in most of the faculty evaluation system are ill defined; neither they are balanced nor in conformity with objectives of higher education as defined by UGC i.e. teaching, research and extension. Moreover, factors need to be clearly described, so that all raters have some sort of behaviour in mind. Further, unless all raters agrees on how such terms as integrity or intellectual level could be dealt objectively, their final rating simply cannot be compared.

3. The Rater' Error

In fact, a completely error free performance appraisal can only be an ideal model; the actual performance might be something less than the optimum. Based on the contribution of several behavioral scientists a number of factors can be isolated that can significantly impede the objective evaluation.

i.   **Leniency Error:** Every evaluator has his own value system, which acts as a standard against which appraisals are made. Relative to the true or actual performance on individual exhibits, some evaluators mark high and others low. Former is referred to as positive leniency error and latter as negative leniency error. When evaluators are positively lenient in their appraisal, an individual performance becomes overstated; similarly a negative error understates the performance.

ii. **First Impression:** Raters may identify some specific features of the teacher and quickly form an overall impression about him. The identified qualities and features may not provide adequate base for appraisal.

iii. **Halo and Horn Error:** The halo or horn effect is the tendency to rate high or low on all factors due to impression of a high or low rating on some specific factors. In halo error the entire appraisal is based on one perceived quality of an individual, on the other hand, horn error is attributed to one negative quality or feature perceived, this results in overall lower rating than may be warranted.

iv. **Stereo Typing:** It refers to standard mental picture that an individual holds about a person because of that person's caste, region, sex, age or other features.

v.   **Central Tendency:** In most cases the raters require to justify if the assessment is very poor or outstanding, so raters rate most people as average, as it does not require any clarification or justification.

vi. **Latest behaviour and Spillover Error:** The principal or chairman of the department or Registrar of the university may be influenced by most recent behaviour of the teacher ignoring the commonly demonstrated behaviour during the entire appraisal period.   Spillover error allows the past performance to influence the evaluation of present performance.

4. Lack of Feed Back and Performance Standard

Absence of these two aspects causes significant setbacks to the appraisal system. Performance standards altogether absent in most of the government colleges and universities in Karnataka state.

Need for SET

Reporting in 1986, on the pay scale of University and college teachers the Mehrotra committee had made several important recommendations in order to ensure the accountability of teachers. One of them was student assessment of teachers. The Rastogi committee reiterated this proposal in 1997. Rastogi rightly said that there was no further time to lose or even to introduce it selectively or gradually; instead it should be introduced right way.

In the Western countries, Student assessment of teachers (through a proforma administered after every semester) is used for two purposes. One is to find out what students think about the instruction being imparted to them and the extent to which they profit from it and the other is to use this input not only for academic promotions but also to determine how much raise in salary is to be given to particular teacher. Unlike our country, there is no fixed scale of pay for most academics neither in that country, nor in the rate of increment certain or predetermined. Everything depends upon the performance of the teacher. One way of judging his performance is to find out what students have to say about him. Peer judgment is also given a certain degree of weight age.

Attitudes of Teachers towards Evaluation of their Performance by Students (SET):

Table- 5.1

Distribution of Teachers According to Different Issues Related to Student Evaluation of Teachers (SET)

SL. No.	Issues	SA	A	UD	DA	SDA
1.	Students should not evaluate the teacher	12 (7.9)	24 (15.8)	12 (7.9)	67 (44.1)	37 (24.3
2.	Students are the best judges of their teachers.	43 (28.3)	86 (56.6)	6 (3.9)	12 (7.9)	5 (3.3)
3.	Students are mature to judge their teachers.	12 (7.9)	92 (60.5)	16 (10.5)	20 (13.2)	12 (7.9)
4.	SET will be dangerous for institution having internal assessment marks.	12 (7.9)	18 (11.8)	20 (13.2)	86 (56.6)	16 (10.5)
5.	Student will evaluate teachers on the basis of popularity and grading stringency.	37 (24.3)	43 (28.3)	28 (18.4)	32 (21.1)	12 (7.9)
6.	The result of the evaluation to be made known open.	43 (28.3)	92 (60.5)	10 (6.6)	5 (3.3)	2 (1.3)
7.	Evaluation will affect autonomy of the teachers.	13 (8.6)	18 (11.8)	7 (4.6)	101 (66.4)	13 (8.6)
8.	Evaluation will reduce status difference between students and teachers	8 (5.3)	61 (40.1)	7 (4.6)	70 (46.1)	6 (3.9)
9.	SET should be a continuous process.	30 (19.7)	90 (59.2)	13 (8.6)	13 (8.6)	6 (3.9)
10.	Evaluation will make the teachers less demanding	13 (8.6)	30 (19.7)	20 (13.2)	73 (48.0)	16 (10.5)
11.	The most important purpose of SET is to improve motivational level of teachers	24 (15.8)	110 (72.4)	18 (11.8)	-	-
12.	Evaluation would have negative effect on teaching as teachers would lose confidence to face students who have rated them low	25 (16.4)	29 (19.1)	6 (3.9)	74 (48.7)	18 (11.9)

13.	Evaluation will be a mockery of the teachers and teaching profession.	13 (8.6)	18 (11.8)	21 (13.8)	89 (58.6)	12 (7.9)
14.	Evaluation would be used by the administrator as stick to humiliate teachers.	17 (11.2)	13 (8.6)	24 (15.8)	74 (28.7)	24 (15.7)
15.	Only students can objectively evaluate teachers as they sit in the class for longer duration.	24 (15.8)	77 (50.7)	16 (10.5)	14 (9.3)	18 (11.8)
16.	Evaluation may help the teachers in knowing and improving the weaknesses.	30 (19.7)	92 (60.5)	16 (10.5)	14 (9.3)	-
17.	Evaluation will help to know where the teachers stand in the eyes of the students.	18 (11.8)	102 (67.2)	20 (13.1)	12 (7.9)	-
18.	Evaluation will enhance the teachers self respect and sense of responsibility.	6 (3.9)	109 (71.7)	12 (7.9)	25 (16.5)	-
19.	To check the deteriorating quality of classroom teaching students must be given the right to evaluate the teacher's effectiveness.	29 (19.9)	78 (51.3)	30 (19.7)	8 (5.3)	7 (4.6)
20.	Student rating of the teachers shall be more objective than other alternatives	18 (11.8)	72 (51.3)	36 (23.7)	18 (11.8)	8 (5.3)

Source: Field Survey

Table - 5.1 shows the responses towards various queries put on the issues of the university teachers evaluation by the students. The first question put to the teacher respondents has been 'students should not evaluate teachers'. The responses indicate that, of 152 respondents 104 (68.4 per cent) disagreed to the statement. Most of the respondents agreed to evaluate their performance by students. However 26.7 per cent of respondents agreed to the statement and opined that students should not evaluate. Most of them justified their view point with numerous examples indicating that it will be detrimental due to various reasons highlighted in the forth coming discussion. Majority of the respondent 129 out of 152 (84.9 per cent) agreed to the statement that 'students are the best judges of their teachers'. Only 21.1 per cent of the teachers disagreed with statement that the 'students are mature enough to evaluate the teacher'. To the query regarding student evaluation process may prove to the dangerous for the institutions having internal assessment system about 2/3 of the respondents disagreed. More than 50.0 per cent of the respondents contended that students would evaluate them on the basis of their popularity and grading stringency. To the statement regarding autonomy of the teachers 66.4 per cent maintained that this process would not undermine the autonomy of the teachers. Majority of the respondents (88.8 per cent) agreed to the results of the evaluation made known to open. Among the other notable reasons bearing negative aspects are that evaluation will reduce the status difference between students and teachers (45.4 per cent), evaluation will make the teachers less demanding (28.3 per cent), will reduce the confidence of the teachers on the lower side (35.5 per cent) and evaluation process will make a mockery of teaching profession (20.4 per cent). On the positive side, most of the respondents (134 out of 152) opined that the evaluations process may help as a motivational factor, will help the teachers to know and overcome their weakness (80.3 per cent), will enhance the teachers respect (75.7 per cent), and will be helpful in checking the deteriorating quality of class room teaching (70.4 per cent).

Measurement and Assessment of Teachers Attitudes towards SET

To study the attitude of teachers towards evaluation of their performance by students, a five-point opinion survey scale was developed. The respondents were asked to indicate their perceived degree of agreement or disagreement in respect of each of the twenty statements. Every statement has been rated by the teachers on a five-point scale form strongly Agree (SA), Agree (A), Undecided (UD), and Disagree (DA), to strongly disagree (SDA). The responses to the positive and negative statements were scored 5, 4,3,2,1 and 1, 2,3,4,5 respectively. Half of the items were negatively phrased and, thus, reverse- scored. Accordingly, the possible range of scores was between 20 and 100. High scores indicate the higher level of agreement towards student evaluation of their performance. For a meaningful analysis, the total possible range of scores was split into two categories.

Up to 74: Below average

Above 74: Above average.

Table – 5.2

Teacher's Attitudes towards Student Evaluation

Range of Scores	Levels of Attitude	Number	Percentage
Below 74	Below Average	60	39.5
Above 74	Above Average	92	60.5
	Mean = 74.41 and S.D = 9.55	152	100.00

Source: Field Survey

134

Form the above table, it is clear that out of 152 respondents 60 (39.5 per cent) perceived and reported below average level of attitude towards student evaluation of their performance. Whereas, the respondents reporting above average levels of agreement towards student evaluation of teachers accounted for 60.5 per cent. This trend clearly indicated that most of the university teachers agreed towards student evaluation of their performance.

Mean Scores of the Teachers According to their Organizational Characteristics

Table - 5.3 reveals that, the University teacher's attitude mean scores towards SET (student's evaluation of teacher's performance) according to their organizational characteristics. The overall attitude scores of teachers towards SET were found to be positive as their mean score of 3.72 was more than the neutral score of 3.00. Form the close observation of table –5.3, it is clearly indicated that, four star universities, having more than 300 teaching staff members, older universities (above 30 years) and having student enrolment greater than 3000, are reported more than the overall mean scores (3.72). Whereas the mean attitude score of teachers from five star (3.71) and three star universities (3.67), having number of teaching faculties less than 300 (3.63), age of the universities less than 30 years (3.68) and less than 3000 student enrolment (3.66) were found to be slightly less than the overall attitude mean scores i.e (3.72).

Table - 5.3

Attitude Mean Scores of Teachers According to their Organizational Characteristics

Organizational Characteristics	Frequency (f)	% age	Mean Score
A. NAAC Status:			
***** (5 Star)	95	62.5	3.71
**** (4 Star)	45	29.6	3.75
*** (3 Star)	12	7.9	3.67
B. Number of Teaching Faculty:			
Below 300	85	55.9	3.63
Above 300	67	44.1	3.76
C. Age of the University (in years):			
Below 30	57	37.5	3.68
Above 30	95	62.5	3.79

	Frequency	%	Mean Score
D. Number of Student Enrolment:			
Below 3000	77	50.7	3.66
Above 3000	75	49.3	3.76

Source: Field Survey

In short, Four star university teachers, having more than 300 teaching faculty members, older university teachers and student enrolment was more than 3000 were found to be higher agreement towards evaluation of their performance by students.

Mean Scores of the Teacher According to their Socio-economic Characteristics:

Table - 5.4

Attitude Mean Scores of Teachers According to their Socio-economic Characteristics

Socio-economic Characteristics	Frequency (f)	% age	Mean Score
A. Age:			
Below Average	72	47.4	3.67
Above Average	80	52.6	3.76
B. Sex:			
Male	118	77.6	3.68
Female	34	22.3	3.83
C. Marital Status:			
Single	14	9.2	3.76
Married	138	90.8	3.71
D. Total Monthly Income:			
Below Average	80	52.6	3.67
Above Average	72	47.4	3.78
E. Family Structure:			
Nuclear	134	88.2	3.71
Extended	18	11.8	3.73
F. House Hold Earner Status:			
Single earner	102	67.1	3.69
More than one earner	50	32.9	3.77

G. Family Size			
Below Average	46	30.3	3.74
Above Average	106	69.7	3.70
H. Distance form Dwelling House to Work Place:			
Below Average	80	52.6	3.73
Above Average	72	47.4	3.69

Source: Field Survey

Table-5.4 shows, the mean Attitude scores of the university teachers towards SET according to their socio-economic characteristics. Among those university teachers reported mean score was less than over all attitude mean scores were found in the age group of less than 42 years (3.67), male respondents (3.68), married (3.71), total monthly income had less than `. 25,000 (3.68), live in nuclear family structure (3.71), single house hold earner (3.69), having family members more than 4 (3.70), distance from dwelling house to work place is more than 5 k.m (3.69). Whereas, the university teachers reported above the mean scores were found in the age group of above 42 years, female respondents, unmarried, monthly income more than Rs 25,000, live in the extended family, more than one house hold earner and having family size less than 4 members.

Attitude Mean Scores of the Teachers According to their Career Factors

As seen in the table 5.5, Professor and Associate Professor respondents with job experience of more than 15 years, having PhD qualification, work load per week less than 12 hours, and commerce and science faculty members have reported not only positive attitude towards evaluation of their performance by students but also their mean score was more than the overall mean stores (3.72).

Table - 5.5

Attitude Means Scores of Teachers According to their Career

Career Profile	Frequency (f)	% age	Mean Score
A. Designation:			
Professor	45	29.6	3.74
Associate Professor	47	30.9	3.81
Assistant Professor	60	39.5	3.62
B. Work Experience (in years):			
Below Average	77	50.7	3.66
Above Average	75	49.3	3.78
C. Work Load (in hours per week):			
Below 12	57	37.5	3.79
Above 12	95	62.5	3.70
D. Qualification:			
Ph.D. holders	130	85.5	3.73
Non-Ph.D. holders	22	14.5	3.65
E. Faculty (Department):			
Arts or Humanities	56	36.8	3.62
Commerce and Management	36	23.7	3.73
Science	60	39.5	3.80

Source: Field Survey

Relationship between SET Attitude Scores and Organizational, Socio-economic and Career Profile of the Respondents

The major results and discussions regarding the association between SET Attitudes scores of the respondents and Organizational, Socio-economic, career related factors are presented in the following section. Important variables considered for this analysis include: NAAC status of the respondents employing universities, age of the universities, size of the universities based on the number of teaching staff member, student enrolments in the universities, age of the respondents, sex of the respondent, marital status, total monthly income, type of family structure, family size, house hold earner status, distance from dwelling place to work place, designation wise, work experience, work load per week, status of the doctoral research work and the department in which respondent work.

Relationship between SET Attitude Scores and Organizational Characteristics

Table – 5.6 shows the relationship between the SET Attitudes scores of the university teachers and the characteristics of their employing universities.

Out of 152 respondents 95 were belonging to the universities, which have 5 star NAAC status. Out of 95 respondents who belong to 5 stars NAAC status universities 38 (40.0 per cent) perceived below average level of SET attitude scores. Similarly, out of 45 respondents 17 (37.8 per cent) in found in 4 star universities reported below average level of SET attitude scores. Two-way classification of data was made to test the significance of association between the SET attitude scores and NAAC status of the respondents employing universities. The calculated chi- square value (0.0893) was found to be less than table value (5.991) at 5 per cent level significance for 2 degree of freedom. Therefore it could be inferred that there is no significant association between the SET attitude scores of the respondents and NAAC of their employing universities.

As far as the age of the universities and SET attitude scores are concerned, out of 57 respondents 22 (38.6 per cent) reported below average SET attitude scores were found in the less than 30 years age of the universities. Similar proportions were also found in the above 30 years aged universities. This trend clearly indicated that there is no statistically significant association between these two variables ($\chi^2 = 0.0293$).

Table – 5.6

Relationship between SET Attitude Scores and Organizational Characteristics

Organizational Characteristics	SET Attitude Scores of the University Teachers			χ^2 value
	Below Average	Above Average	Total	
A. NAAC Status:				
***** (5 Star)	38 (40.0)	57 (60.00)	95 (100.0)	
**** (4 Star)	17 (37.8)	28 (62.2)	45 (100.0)	0.089
*** (3 Star)	5 (41.7)	7 (58.3)	12 (100.0)	
Total	60 (39.5)	92 (60.5)	152 (100.0)	

139

B. Age of the Universities (in years):				
Below average (< 30)	22 (38.6)	35 (61.4)	57 (100.0)	
Above average (> 30)	38 (40.0)	57 (60.0)	95 (100.0)	0.029
Total	60 (39.5)	92 (60.5)	152 (100.0)	
C. Number of Teaching Faculty:				
Below Average (< 300)	35 (41.2)	50 (58.8)	85 (100)	
Above Average (> 300)	25 (37.3)	42 (62.7)	67 (100.0)	0.234
Total	60 (39.5)	92 (60.5)	152 (100.0)	
D. Number of Students Enrolment:				
Below Average (< 3000)	28 (38.9)	44 (61.1)	72 (100.0)	
Above Average (> 3000)	32 (40.0)	48 (60.0)	80 (100.0)	0.019
Total	60 (39.5)	92 (60.5)	152 (100.0)	

Source: Field Survey

Finally, the association between size of the universities based on the number of teaching faculty members, student enrolment and the SET attitude scores reveals that there is no significant association at 5 per cent level.

In short, the organizational characteristics of the respondents employing universities and their attitude towards student evaluation of their performance (SET) are not associated.

Socio-Economic Characteristics and SET Attitude Scores

The association between socio-economic characteristics of the respondents and student evaluation of teachers (SET) attitude scores are given in the table – 5.7. Among those are in the age group of above average, 40 (55.6 per cent) out of 72 reported above average level of attitudes towards the evaluation of their performance by student. Similarly, out of 80 respondents who belong to the above average group 52 respondents (65.0 per cent) perceived above average attitude scores. Two-way classifications of data were made to test the significant of association between the SET attitude scores of the university teachers and

140

their age. The calculated chi-square value (1.414) was found to be less that he table value (3.841) at 5 per cent of level of significance for 1-degree freedom.

Similarly, the association between the sex, marital status, total monthly income of the respondents, family structure, household earners status, family size of the respondents, distance form dwelling place to work place and their attitude scores towards student evaluation of their performance (SET) are not statistically significant. In all these cases the calculated value of chi-square was found to be much lesser than the table value.

In short, the socio-economic characteristics of the respondents could not influence to their perceived level of student evaluation (SET).

Table – 5.7

Association between Socio-economic Characteristics and SET Attitude

Socio-economic Characteristics		SET Attitude Scores of the University Teachers			χ^2 value
		Below Average	Above Average	Total	
A. Age:					
Below Average		32 (44.4)	40 (55.6)	72 (100.0)	
Above Average		28 (35.0)	52 (65.0)	80 (100.0)	1.414
	Total	60 (39.5)	92 (60.5)	152 (100.0)	
B. Sex:					
Male		49 (41.5)	69 (58.5)	118 (100.0)	
Female		11 (32.4)	23 (67.6)	34 (100.0)	0.929
	Total	60 (39.5)	92 (60.5)	152 (100.0)	
C. Marital Status:					
Single		4 (28.6)	10 (71.4)	14 (100.0)	
Married		56 (40.6)	82 (59.4)	138 (100.0)	0.767
	Total	60 (39.5)	92 (60.5)	152 (100.0)	

D. Monthly Income:				
Below Average	33 (41.3)	47 (58.7)	80 (100.0)	
Above Average	27 (37.5)	45 (62.5)	72 (100.0)	0.223
Total	60 (39.5)	92 (60.5)	152 (100.0)	

E. Family Structure:				
Nuclear	54 (40.3)	80 (59.7)	134 (100.0)	
Extended	6 (33.3)	12 (66.7)	18 (100.0)	0.322
Total	60 (39.5)	92 (60.5)	152 (100.0)	

F. House Hold Earner Status:				
One Earner	41 (40.2)	61 (59.8)	102 (100.0)	
More than One Earner	19 (38.0)	31 (62.0)	50 (100.0)	0.067
Total	60 (39.5)	92 (60.5)	152 (100.0)	

G. Family size:				
Below Average	18 (39.1)	28 (60.9)	46 (100.0)	
Above Average	42 (39.6)	64 (60.4)	106 (100.0)	0.003
Total	60 (39.5)	92 (60.5)	152 (100.0)	

H. Distance from Dwelling Place to Work Place (in km):				
Below Average	34 (42.5)	46 (57.5)	80 (100.0)	
Above Average	26 (36.1)	46 (63.9)	72 (100.0)	0.647
Total	60 (39.5)	92 (60.5)	152 (100.0)	

Source: Field Survey

Table – 5.8

Association between Career Profile of the Respondents and Their SET Attitude Scores

Career Profile of the Respondents	SET Attitude Scores of the University Teachers			χ^2 value
	Below Average	Above Average	Total	
A. Designation:				
Professor	21 (46.7)	24 (53.3)	45 (100.0)	
Associate Professor	13 (27.7)	34 (56.7)	47 (100.0)	4.094
Assistant Professor	26 (43.3)	34 (56.7)	60 (100.0)	
Total	60 (39.5)	92 (60.5)	152 (100.0)	
B. Work Experience (in years):				
Below Average	30 (40.0)	47 (60.0)	77 (100.0)	
Above Average	30 (39.0)	45 (61.0)	75 (100.0)	0.017
Total	60 (39.5)	92 (60.5)	152 (100.0)	
C. Work Load Per Week (in hours):				
Below Average	32 (56.1)	25 (43.9)	57 (100.0)	
Above Average	28 (29.5)	67 (70.5)	95 (100.0)	10.603
Total	60 (39.5)	92 (60.5)	152 (100.0)	
D. Status of Ph.D. Work:				
Ph.D. Degree Holders	53 (40.8)	77 (59.2)	130 (100.0)	
Non Ph.D. Degree Holders	7 (31.8)	15 (68.2)	22 (100.0)	0.630
Total	60 (39.5)	92 (60.5)	152 (100.0)	

E. Faculty/Department:				
Arts	24 (42.9)	32 (57.1)	56 (100.0)	
Commerce	15 (41.7)	21 (58.3)	36 (100.0)	0.843
Science	21 (35.0)	39 (65.0)	60 (100.0)	
Total	60 (39.5)	92 (60.5)	152 (100.0)	

Source: Field Survey

Table 5.8 reveals the relationship between the career profile of the respondents and their perception towards student evaluation of teacher's performance (SET).

As far as the designation of the respondents and their perceived level of SET attitude scores are concerned, of 45 professor respondents 46.7 per cent perceived below average level of attitudes towards SET. Similarly out of 60 Assistant Professor respondents 43.3 per cent perceived below average level of attitude towards SET. The calculated value of Chi-square (4.094) was found to be less than table value (5.991) at 5 per cent level of significance for 2 degree of freedom. Hence, it could be concluded that there is no significant association between the SET attitude scores of the respondents and their designation in the university.

A similar trend could also be seen in respect of the relationship between work experience of the respondents and their perceived level of SET scores. Out of 77 respondents those had less than 14 years of work experience 47 (61.0 per cent) reported above average SET attitude scores. The similar proportion of respondents reported above average SET Attitude scores had work experience of more than 14 years.

The calculated chi-square value (0.0176) was found to be less than table value (3.841) for 1 degree of freedom. Hence, it could be inferred that there is no significance association between job experience and SET attitude scores of the respondents.

In contrast, the workload per week (direct class room teaching) and SET attitude scores of the respondents was found to be associated. Out of 152 respondents 57 were engaging less than average number of class work per week. Among those engaging below average number of hours of class work per week 56.1 per cent perceived and reported below average level of attitude scores towards SET. Whereas, out of 95 respondents who engaging above average number of class hours per week 67 (70.5 per cent) reported above average level of attitude scores of SET. Two-way classifications of data were made to test the significance of association between these two variables. The calculated chi-square value (10.603) was found to be higher than the table value (3.841) at 1 per cent level of significance.

There is no significant association between the status of the Ph.D work, department in which respondents work, and their attitude scores towards SET.

In short, among the various career related aspects of the respondents considered for this study only the work load per week and their Attitude towards student evaluation of teachers (SET) are related. Whereas, designation of the respondents, work experience, status of the Ph.D. work and department of the respondents could not influence to their SET attitude scores.

In summary, more than 68.0 per cent of the respondents held that students are capable to evaluate teachers. Majority of the university teachers (84.9 per cent) admitted that students are the best judges of their teachers. Majority of the respondents (88.8 per cent) agreed to the results of the evaluation made known to open. Most of the respondents opined that the evaluation process may help them as a motivational factor (88.2 per cent), to know an overcome their weakness (80.3 per cent), and will enhance their respect (75.7 per cent). Only small proportion of them (28.3 per cent) had the fear that evaluation will make the teachers less demanding, will reduce the confidence of the teachers on the lower side, and evaluate them on the basis of grading stringency/popularity.

Irrespective of the organizational, demographic and career aspects of the respondents, all are perceived and reported above moderate level (3.00) towards student's evaluation of their performance.

Based on the foregoing results and discussions the fourth hypothesis has been accepted (H₄) – **"There is no association between organizational, demographic, and career related aspects of the respondents and their perceived levels of attitude towards student evaluation of teachers (SET) performance"**.

Reference

1. Millman, J., (1981), "Hand Book of Teachers Evaluation," Beverly Hills: Sage.
2. Mookerji, R.K., (1969), "Ancient Indian Education: Brahmanical and Buddist," (4th edition), Delhi: Motilal Banarsidass.
3. Sweeny, J., and Manatt, R.P., (1986), "teachers Evaluation and Performance Assessment," R.A. Berk (Ed), pp. 446-468.

CHAPTER - VI

FINDINGS, SUGGESTIONS AND CONCLUSION

In Universities, attitudes of the teachers are important because they affect job behaviour. The various job-related attitudes are job satisfaction, job involvement and organizational commitment. This study also includes the attitudes of the University teachers towards Student Evaluation of Teachers (SET) performance.

Altitude of the employees depends on attitudes towards objects, people or events. Attitudes are evaluative statements or judgments that employees hold about various aspects of their job and job environment. In the previous chapters an attempt has been made to study the issue of "Job Attitude of University Teachers" on various aspects of job. This chapter devoted to present a brief summary of what has been discussed and analyzed in the earlier chapters.

The present findings are based on a sample of 152 university teachers (60 Assistant Professor, 47 Associate Professors, 45 Professors) employed in six conventional universities in Karnataka state. Out of total number of respondents, 62.5, 29.6 and 7.9 percent were working at five star, four star, and three star universities respectively. These university teachers were broadly categorized into three departments, 36.9 per cent come under Arts or social science, 23.7 percent work in commerce and management, and 39.4 percent serve in the science department. The overall mean-age of the respondents was 42 years. Position wise, the mean age increased, it was 36 years at the Assistant Professor's level, 43 years at the Associate Professor Level and 49 years at the Professor level. At the same time the overall mean length of service was found to be15 years, which also increases level wise. Eight years of experience at the Assistant Professor level, 16 years at the Associate Professor Level and 24 years at the Professor level.

The overall average monthly income was recorded `. 68,882. The major findings of the study are as follows.

Measurement of Job Attitudes:

1. Most of the university teachers perceived moderate to high-level job satisfaction. (Table-3.1)

2. 90 respondents Out of 152 (59.2 per cent) perceived moderate level of job involvement. (Table-3.12)

3. Around 50.0 per cent of the respondents reported moderate degree of Organizational commitment. Majority of the Professor respondents reported high degree of continuance and moderate degree of normative commitment. (Table-3.13)

Specific Job Satisfaction:

4. All most every respondent reported their perceived level of satisfaction above moderate for various specific aspects of job except for supervision, mentoring, library facilities, clerical assistance, and teamwork.

5. Higher fulfilled facets of job are work- itself, pay, achievement, responsibility, status, professional growth etc.

6. 'Clerical assistance' and 'work itself' have been perceived as lowest and highest satisfied aspects of job.

7. The Professor respondent reported the lowest satisfaction for clerical assistance followed by library facilities, mentoring and supervision. The Associate Professor respondents perceived lower degree of satisfaction for supervision, working condition, mentoring, library facilities, clerical assistance and teamwork. Teamwork, mentoring and clerical assistance are lowest fulfilled aspects of job for Assistant Professor Respondent.

8. The satisfaction level for most of the aspects of job and its environment decreased from the Professor respondents to the Associate Professor and from the Associate Professor to the Assistant Professor respondents.

9. The respondents of all the six universities irrespective of NAAC status have reported higher level of satisfaction for work itself, responsibility,

achievement, pay, status, and professional growth. A lower level of satisfaction is experienced for supervision, mentoring, clerical assistance and teamwork.

Expectation from Job and its Environment:

10. For every aspect of job and its environment the respondent's expectation is above moderate level. The aspects, for which higher expectations were claimed are library facility, achievement, inter-personal relation, research work, working conditions, work itself, university policy and administration.

11. The expectation from Job and its environment rises from the Assistant Professor to the Associate Professor and from Associate Professor to Professor Respondent for pay, recognition, advancement, Creativity, research work, and status. Whereas this trend was reverse in case of supervision, job security.

12. NAAC status-wise analysis comes out with the fact that the respondents from five star universities have reported the high level of expectation for all aspects of job except supervision and status. The respondents of the four star and three star universities indicates highest expectations for working conditions.

GAP in Job Satisfaction:

13. Wider gaps have been found irrespective of position of the respondents and NAAC status of the University Library Facilities, teamwork, clerical assistance, university policy and administration, interpersonal relations, mentoring, research work, and advancement.

Association between Overall Job Satisfaction and Specific Job Satisfaction:

14. A positive association was found between overall job satisfaction and achievement, recognition, advancement, work itself, professional growth, responsibility, creativity, involvement and research work, university policy and administrative, pay, and working conditions,.

Association among Job Attitudes:

15. In the light of inter-correlations among job related attitudes observed that, a moderate positive relationship between the university teachers perception of

overall job satisfaction and job involvement (r= 0.55). The association between Overall job satisfaction and Organizational commitment of the university teachers was found to be positive but weak (r= 0.13). Similarly the relationship between job involvement and Organizational commitment was found to be positive (r=0.27).

Determinants of Job Attitudes:

16. Majority of the university teachers reported high levels of overall job satisfaction, job involvement, and organizational commitment belonged to five stars NAAC accredited universities; those universities aged more than 30 years.

17. A significant number of university teachers perceiving high degree of job satisfaction were employed in those universities having more than 300 teaching faculty members. Whereas, most of them experiencing high levels of job involvement and organizational commitment were found in those universities employing less than 300 teaching faculty members.

18. Similarly, most of the respondents reporting high degree of job satisfaction and organizational commitment were identified in those universities enrolling more than 3000 students. While, majority of them experiencing high degree of job involvement were found in those university enrolled less than 3000 students.

19. As far as the socio- economic characteristics of the university teachers are concerned, the majority of the University teachers reporting high degree of job satisfaction, job involvement, and organizational commitment were above the age of 42 years, were enjoying married life, had an monthly income of more than `50,000, belongs to nuclear families, having a smaller family of fewer than 4 members and distance from dwelling place to work place is less than 5 K.M.

20. Most of them experiencing high level of overall job satisfaction and organizational commitment were male employees. Whereas, a greater proportion of the University teachers reporting high level of job involvement were female.

21. Similarly, a sizable proportion of them reporting high degree of job satisfaction and job involvement belong to single-earner household. While, a significant

number of them reporting high level of organizational commitment represented more than one-earner household.

22. With regard to the career-related factors, a greater proportion of the University teachers perceiving high degree of job satisfaction, job involvement and organizational commitment had a job experience of more than 15 years, having Ph.D. degree qualification.

23. Similarly, about one-half of the University teachers indicating high degree of job satisfaction and job involvement were professor respondents. While, about fifty percent of the respondents reporting high degree of organizational commitment were Assistant Professor Respondents. There exists a association between job attitudes and number of hour of work load per week.

Student Evaluation of Teachers Performance (SET)

24. This study led to the conclusion that more than 68.0 per cent of the respondents held that student are capable to evaluate teachers.

25. Majority of the university teachers (84.9 per cent) admitted that students are the best judges of their teacher.

26. Only little more than 21.0 per cent of the respondents indicated that student are not mature enough to evaluate the teachers.

27. More than 50.0 per cent of the respondents contented that student will evaluate them on the basis of their popularity and grading stringency.

28. Majority of the respondents (88.8 per cent) agreed to the results of the evaluation made known to open.

29. Most of the respondents opined that the evaluation process may help them as a motivational factor (88.2 per cent), to know and overcome their weakness, (80.3 per cent), will enhance the teacher respect (75.7 per cent).

30. Only small proportion of them (28.3 per cent) had the fear that evaluation will make the teachers less demanding, and will reduce the confidence of the teachers on the lower side (35.5 per cent).

31. It should also be noted that most of the university teachers (60.5 per cent) perceived and reported above average levels of agreement towards student evaluation of teacher's performance.

32. Irrespective of the Organizational, socio-economic and career aspects, all respondents perceived above neutral score (3.00) towards student evaluation. Whereas, four star university respondents, having more than 300 teaching faculty members, old university teacher respondents and student enrolment more than 3000 university respondents reported more than mean scores (3.72) towards student evaluation.

33. The university teachers reported above the mean scores (3.72) were found in the age group of 42 years, female respondents, unmarried, total monthly income more than ` 50,000, live in the extended family, more than one house hold earner.

34. Professor and Associate Professor respondents, having job experience of more than 15 years, doctoral degree holders, engaging less than 12 hours of direct class room teaching per week reported above mean scores (3.72) towards student evaluation of teacher performance.

35. Organizational, Socio economic and Career aspects of the respondents and their perceived levels of student evaluation are not associated".

Suggestions:

Based on the findings of this study certain general and specific suggestions are presented below to realign the job attitudes of university teachers.

1. **Universities should conduct periodic attitude survey of their employees**. It provides useful data and information as to how employees feel about their job, facets of job, and job environment. Appropriately and timely act upon the findings of job attitude survey helps the university and employees to utilize their unique talents and competencies both effectively and efficiently. It helps the university authorities to know their employees' level of overall job satisfaction, job involvement and organizational commitment. The universities will have to examine, understand and address various job-related issues faced by the employees.

2. **In order to raise the level of overall job satisfaction of the university teachers,** the university need to address certain specific aspects of job such as, provide all types of support and facilities to individual teachers for professional growth, recognize teachers outstanding and excellent work, delegate more authority in turn it increases their responsibility, and promotion or advancement should be given to the teachers when its due.

3. **To keep the university teachers minimum level of job dissatisfaction,** the university should adopt teacher-friendly policy and administration, arrange mentoring facilities to the young teachers, provide modern research oriented library facilities, support and encourage teamwork, and clerical staff should be trained in such a way that they are supportive to the teaching faculty in the department.

4. **Universities should maintain optimum level of student-teacher ratio** to increase the level of job involvement of the university teachers. In light of this there is an association between job involvement and student enrollment. It is advisable to the university authorities either to recruit regular or guest faculties in the department or to right size the student enrollment.

5. **Universities are advisable to see that their employees are residing nearer to the universities** as attitudes of teachers and distances from their dwelling houses to work place are related. This can be achieved by providing accommodation nearer to the universities.

6. **The System of Student Evaluation of Teachers (SET) performance will have to be comprehensively and thoroughly Indianised.** Students would have to be educated about the objectives and process of SET in the full sense

Model Questionnaire for Student Evaluation of Teachers (SET) Performance

Dear Student,

You are required to assess the performance of teachers on the basis of the questions given below. Mark your assessment by putting a tick mark ( ) against your choice of answer. Please read the questions carefully and answer them honestly and sincerely.

Q. No	Questions	5	4	3	2	1
1.	How punctual is the teacher in engaging the classes?	Extremely punctual	Very punctual	Quite punctual	Not very punctual	Not at all punctual
2.	How sincere is the teacher towards teaching?	Extremely sincere	Very sincere	Quite sincere	Not very sincere	Not at all sincere
3.	How would you rate the subject knowledge of teacher?	Extremely knowledgeable	Very knowledgeable	Quit knowledgeable	Not very knowledgeable	Not at all knowledgeable
4.	How neat is the appearance of the teacher?	Extremely neat	Very neat	Quit neat	Not very neat	Not at all neat
5.	How effective is the teacher in communicating ideas clearly?	Extremely effective	Very effective	Quit effective	Not effective	Not at all effective
6.	How interesting is the class of teacher?	Extremely interesting	Very interesting	Quit interesting	Not very interesting	Not at all interesting
7.	How prepared is the teacher for each class?	Extremely prepared	Very prepared	Quit prepared	Not very prepared	Not at all prepared
8.	How satisfied are you with the way in which portions are covered?	Highly satisfied	Satisfied	Neutral	Not satisfied	Not at all satisfied

154

9.	How innovative are the teaching methods adopted by the teacher?	E tremely innovative	Very innovative	Quit innovative	Not very innovative	Not at all innovative
10.	How impartial is the teacher towards all students?	E tremely impartial	Very impartial	Quit impartial	Not very impartial	Not at all impartial
11.	How approachable is the teacher for help and guidance?	E tremely approachable	Very approachable	Quit approachable	Not very approachable	Not at all approachable
12.	How involved is the teacher in e tra/co-curricular activities?	E tremely involved	Very involved	Quit involved	Not very involved	Not at all involved
13.	How available is the teacher on the campus during class /after class hour?	Almost always available	Always available	Quit some time available	Not always available	Never available

155

Conclusion:

Overall job satisfaction of the university teachers tends to be significantly associated with their perceived levels of specific job satisfaction viz., teaching, research, professional growth, recognition, creativity, etc. The university teacher reported highest and lowest level of satisfaction as the work itself and clerical assistance. There exists a positive association between overall job satisfaction and job involvement, job satisfaction and organizational commitment, job involvement and organizational commitment of the university teachers. Organizational, Demographic and Career-related factors determine university teacher's perception of job satisfaction, job involvement and organizational commitment. The university teachers agreed towards student evaluation of their performance. Organizational, Demographic and Career factors do not influence to their attitude towards student evaluation of their performance.

The findings and conclusions of this study cannot be generalized because of regional, national and cross-cultural differences. Hence, future researcher can examine by undertaking a comparative study of two samples selecting from two different states or different cultures.

Future researcher also examines the relationship between job related attitudes and its outcome, such as job performance, absenteeism/ turnover, organizational citizenship behaviour (OCB), life satisfaction, and family involvement of the respondents.

ABOUT THE AUTHOR

Dr. Ishwara P is currently working as Associate Professor in the Department of studies and research in commerce, Mangalore University. He did his post graduate degree in commerce from the same university in the year 1995. Then he did his Doctoral work in the Kuvempu University in 2005.   He has 17 years of teaching and research experience. He has published more than 50 research papers in both National and International Journals with ISSN. He has also presented 40 research papers in national and International seminars and conferences. He has successfully guided 12 candidates for their M. Phil degree and presently 8 candidates are pursuing their doctoral degree.

www.ingramcontent.com/pod-product-compliance
Lightning Source LLC
Chambersburg PA
CBHW061743270326
41928CB00011B/2357